WITHDRAWN
NDSU

MORE ESSAYS ON GREEK ROMANCES

MORE ESSAYS ON GREEK ROMANCES

BY

ELIZABETH HAZELTON HAIGHT

Professor Emeritus of Latin, Vassar College

NEW YORK

LONGMANS, GREEN AND CO.

M D CCCC XLV

123033

45 - 4291

HAIGHT
MORE ESSAYS ON GREEK ROMANCES

COPYRIGHT · 1945
BY LONGMANS, GREEN AND CO., INC.

ALL RIGHTS RESERVED, INCLUDING THE
RIGHT TO REPRODUCE THIS BOOK, OR
ANY PORTION THEREOF, IN ANY FORM

PUBLISHED SIMULTANEOUSLY IN
THE DOMINION OF CANADA BY
LONGMANS, GREEN AND CO., TORONTO

FIRST EDITION

PA
3267
H32

*This complete copyright edition
is produced in full compliance with
the Government's regulations for
conserving paper and other
essential materials.*

PRINTED IN THE UNITED STATES OF AMERICA

To

MY SISTER

HELEN IVES HAIGHT

The Publication

of this book was made possible

by the

J. LEVERETT MOORE RESEARCH FUND

IN CLASSICS

and the

LUCY MAYNARD SALMON FUND

FOR RESEARCH

established at Vassar College

in 1926

WHEN I published my book, "Essays on The Greek Romances," I found that I had accumulated enough material for another volume. The subject matter of this is heterogeneous, but, I believe, it all supplements and enriches the picture I have already given of the fiction of the early Empire.

The arrangement of the essays perhaps needs some explanation. I have placed the Alexander Romance first, not because of the probable date of the extant version, but because of its type. The romance of the conquering hero, unadulterated by any love motif, seems to antedate the historical romance centered on love if we may trust the indications of the fragments of the Ninus Romance. Moreover, the Alexander Romance is the most important of all in this volume (with the exception of Apuleius' *Metamorphoses*) in its influence on later literature.

After the Alexander Romance, I have grouped together three romances of the spirit, two Christian rivals of the pagan novels of the time, one a romantic biography of a self-sufficient philosopher, Apollonius of Tyana. Following these come two studies in comparative literature, *Apuleius and Boccaccio, Apollonius of Tyre and Shakespeare's "Pericles, Prince of Tyre."* These are discussions of Latin novels, which go back to Greek Romances, illuminated by comparisons with individual imitators.

If John Buchan were still living, I should beg the privilege of sending to him my two books on the Greek Romances. For John Buchan, the best writer of romances in our time, would have appreciated, I feel sure, how significant for their age and in their aspirations these Greek stories are. In a little-read essay, "The Novel and the Fairy Tale," [1] John Buchan showed how deeply rooted in the folk tale the elements of the Victorian novel were. The few good plots or motives for stories he believed to be "the picaresque motive, the story based on extension in space, on the fact that the world is very wide and that there are a great many odd things in it" ; the motive which "Aristotle called *Peripeteia* or Reversal of Fortune," often coupled with his *Anagnorisis* or Recognition ; third, "the Survival of the Unfittest, the victory against odds of the unlikeliest people" ; and, finally, the use of ordinary human beings as characters, accompanied by a great "optimism about human nature," which makes the real purpose of the story the "glorification of the soul of man." All these elements of the folk tale and the great Victorian novels appear in these Greek Romances, for their roots too penetrate to the deepest soil of mother earth and draw from her eternal verities sustenance for the life of her human children.

Once again I wish to make grateful acknowledgments to publishers and authors for permission to quote material. I am indebted to the Harvard University Press, Cambridge, Mass., for its generosity in allowing me to quote freely from volumes in *The Loeb Classical Library,* and for the use of a passage from H. E. Wethey, *Gil de Siloe and his School* ; to the Cambridge University Press for the use of material from T. R. Glover, *Life and Letters in the Fourth Century,* from M. R. James, "Apocrypha

[1] Published by *The English Association,* Pamphlet No. 79, July, 1931, Oxford University Press.

Anecdota" in *Texts and Studies,* vol. II. No. 3, and from
W. W. Tarn in *The Cambridge Ancient History,* vol. VI ;
to the Clarendon Press, Oxford, for the use of material
from J. W. Mackail, *The Approach to Shakespeare,* from
Sir Sidney Lee, *Shakespeare's Pericles,* and from J. S. Phillimore, *Philostratus, in honour of Apollonius of Tyana* ;
to John Murray for the use of a quotation from Sir Sidney
Lee, *A Life of William Shakespeare* ; to Basil Blackwell
for a quotation from Martin Braun, *History and Romance
in Graeco-Oriental Literature* ; to the Oxford University
Press for short quotations from John Buchan, *The Novel
and the Fairy Tale* ; to G. P. Putnam's Sons for the use
of material from William M. Ramsay, *The Church in the
Roman Empire before A.D.* 170 ; to Charles Scribner's
Sons for quotations of passages from the *Ante-Nicene
Fathers* ; to Whittlesey House for the use of passages from
Margaret Webster's *Shakespeare Without Tears* ; to the
Catholic University of America Press for quotations from
Sister M. Rosamond Nugent's dissertation ; and for cour-
teous permissions to make quotations from their books
granted by Mr. Edward Hutton, Professor Alfred R. Bel-
linger, Dr. R. T. Ohl, and Professor Charles G. Osgood.
Also I am indebted to Professor A. J. B. Wace, who in spite
of the difficulties of mail in war time sent me from the
University of Alexandria manuscript copies of his forth-
coming articles on the Serapeum and the Tomb of Alexander, a courtesy which I deeply appreciate.

To Vassar College I owe perennial gratitude. The Library and especially its head, Miss Fanny Borden, con-
tinues to give me the most generous and efficient help and,
moreover, I have been allowed to publish portions of one
of its incunabula. In my study in the Library and in my
own apartment, I am provided with ideal conditions for

research and writing. And I am again indebted to the Research Funds of the college which have made possible the publication of this volume.

After these acknowledgments, I wish to pay a special tribute to John Benbow of Longmans, Green & Co., whose death on February 21, 1944 was a great personal loss to me. Mr. Benbow had helped me bring out my last five books and in that association had given me not only invaluable technical aid, but constant stimulus for new work. A classical scholar himself, whose hobby was the collection of early Greek texts in different types, he showed unfailing interest in my writing. And, a perfectionist in the craft of book-making, he conveyed to me his own ardor for a beautiful format and fair pages as free from flaws as is humanly possible. It was his taste which selected the Baskerville type for my books since it had been used in the printing of the Classics in the Eighteenth Century. He insisted on leisurely processes in proof-reading and index-making so that enjoyment of work would secure success. And he made business correspondence a pleasure by his whimsies and by little hand-written notes at letters' ends. I keep on my desk his book, "Manuscript and Proof," as the best of practical aids for a writer. His encouraging words, his serenity in working, his standard of beauty remain fixed in my memory. It has been my privilege to realize that his spirit lives on in the great House of which he was a representative. Let my final word for him be what he wrote at the completion of one of my books: *"Feliciter explicit."*

CONTENTS

CONTENTS

MORE ESSAYS
ON GREEK ROMANCES

I

THE HISTORY OF ALEXANDER THE GREAT

BY PSEUDO-CALLISTHENES

"ALISAUNDRE's storie is so commune
That everie wight that hath discrecionne,
Hath herde somewhat or al of his fortune." [1]

So wrote Chaucer of the Alexander Romance and he was right, for of all the Greek Romances this so-called History of Alexander the Great was the most popular in after times. Grässe in 1842 calculated that there were eighty versions of the Alexander Romance in twenty-four languages, and later studies have shown that Grässe's figures should be at least doubled.[2] Since I have found no English translation of the Pseudo-Callisthenes, the oldest extant prototype,[3] I wish to publish a rather full summary or paraphrase in order to make the contents more available for students of the history of fiction. I intend to confine myself to the presentation of the Pseudo-Callisthenes story, adding only such setting and interpretations as may serve to elucidate the romance. It would be impossible

---

[1] G. Chaucer, "The Monk's Tale" in The Canterbury Tales, 3821.

[2] Fr. Pfister, "Zur Geschichte der Alexander-tradition und des Alexanderromans," Woch. für Klass. Phil., 1911, no. 42, pp. 1152–53.

[3] Of course, there are early English versions, e. g., "The Prose Life of Alexander" (Thornton Ms.) in Early English Text Society, Original Series, 143, London, 1913 (for 1911). A delightful re-telling of the whole Alexander Romance from various sources is The Story of Alexander told by Robert Steele and drawn by Fred Mason, London, 1894.

in the scope of this book to compare the narrative with the historians and with Plutarch, or to present, even in summary, the vast influence which this had on following centuries.[4]

The historical Greek romance is a type which must have existed early since its influence is seen in the romance of Ninus (First Century B.C.), in the use of historical events and characters in the love romances of the Second and Third Centuries A.D., in the caricature of its travellers' tales in Lucian's *True History*. The great illustration of this type is the Alexander Romance. Now, although the extant Greek version was probably not written until the Third Century A.D., many have thought that it derives from an earlier version written soon after Alexander's death. And this hypothesis would explain the use of historical elements in the love romances. The Ninus Romance, moreover, would be the transitional link between this early historical romance and the later love romances, for it creates a love-story between two famous historical characters, Ninus and Semiramis.[5] Be that as it may, what we have before us to study is a Greek romance called *The History of Alexander the Great*, allegedly written by Callisthenes, but probably written in the Third Century A.D.

The author of this romance is actually unknown. The name Callisthenes appears only in certain manuscripts of the B Family and in Tzetzes.[6] The original Callisthenes was a nephew and pupil of Aristotle who wrote *Hellenica* in ten books and a work on the Deeds of Alex-

[4] For bibliography of the Alexander Romance see *Jahresbericht über der klassischen Altertumswissenschaft*, C. Bursian und W. Kroll, 1910, 147–50, Leipsic, 1911, pp. 196–99 ; C. Bursian und A. Körte, 1915, 170–73, Leipsic, 1917, pp. 214–23.

[5] R. M. Rattenbury in *New Chapters in the History of Greek Literature*, Third Series, Oxford, 1933, edited by J. U. Powell, pp. 220–22.
[6] W. Kroll, *Historia Alexandri Magni* (Pseudo-Callisthenes), vol. I, Berlin, 1926, p. xv.

ander.   As he was an ardent supporter of Alexander, he
was taken into Asia with him, but when he became critical
of Alexander's orientalizing policy, he fell into disgrace
and perished about 327 B.C.   The unknown author of the
Greek romance of Alexander was assumed in certain
manuscripts to be this Callisthenes.[7]

Almost as uncertain as the identity of the author are
the date and the sources of the romance.   A *terminus
ante quem* is set by the Latin translation of Julius Valerius
Polemius, who was possibly the consul of A.D. 338, and
who certainly wrote about that time.[8]   Rohde and Ausfeld would assign the original romance, the kernel of
which they find in Pseudo-Callisthenes, to the late Ptole-
maic period (about 200 B.C., in the time of Ptolemy Epiphanes).   But this assumption seems to date the bulk of
the extant romance too early since certain mistakes and
peculiarities of text and diction would seem to relegate it
to about A.D. 300.[9]   As Ausfeld points out,[10] in text *a*,
which arose at Alexandria, certain episodes point to the
epoch of the Roman emperors.   The story of Candace
points probably to the downfall of a Candace under Augustus, perhaps also to a Roman expedition into Ethiopia
under Nero.[11]   Carthage, which is one of the great cities,
had a new *floruit* in the Empire.   The Alani, who are
referred to in a list of Persians in I. 2, were mentioned
first by Lucan.   And the Favorinus of I. 13 was a philosopher of the time of Trajan and Hadrian.

[7] W. von Christ, *Geschichte der
griechischen Literatur*, umgearbeitet
von W. Schmid und O. Stählin, Mu-
nich, 1912, vol. I, p. 535.

[8] W. Kroll, *op. cit.*, p. viii: *Iuli
Valeri Alexandri Polemi Res Gestae
Alexandri Macedonis*, edited by B.
Kuebler, Leipsic, 1888.

[9] W. Kroll, *op. cit.*, p. xv.

[10] A. Ausfeld, *Der griechische Alex-
anderroman*, nach des verfassers
Tode herausgegeben von W. Kroll,
Leipsic, 1907, pp. 251–52.

[11] Candace is really a title, the
equivalent of *basilissa*. Grace H.
Macurdy, *Vassal-Queens and Some
Contemporary Women in the Roman Empire*, Baltimore, 1937, pp.
132–33.

There is a considerable consensus of opinion that the original romance was written soon after Alexander's death, for some of the material used belongs to a very early tradition. This is proved by papyri fragments. One of these for example dating in the II–I Centuries B.C. describes the visit of Alexander to the Gymnosophists which is related by Pseudo-Callisthenes III. 5–6.[12] The characteristics of this hypothetical early romance are that it is not a folk tale, but it has in it a kernel of true history going back to the good tradition based on Clitarchus.[13] Another theory has been proposed that the original source of Pseudo-Callisthenes was a collection of letters around which the romance was built. (There are thirty-eight letters directly quoted in the story, but of these probably only the one to Aristotle, possibly also the one to Olympias, reflect genuine letters.)

All these conjectures about the author and the date of the Pseudo-Callisthenes romance are as purely hypothetical as are the theories about the period and the nature of the earliest form of the existing story. The different views need to be stated, even if they are not accepted. The historicity of the story cannot be discussed until we have read a full outline of it. Before presenting that I wish to quote what Plutarch said of his own methods in writing his life of Alexander :

"It is not Histories that I am writing, but Lives ; and in the most illustrious deeds there is not always a manifestation of virtue or vice, nay, a slight thing like a phrase or a jest often makes a greater revelation of character than battles where thousands fall, or the greatest armaments, or sieges of cities. Accordingly, just as painters get the likenesses in their portraits from the face and the expression of the eyes, wherein the character shows itself, but

[12] R. M. Rattenbury, *op. cit.*, pp. 220–22.

[13] W. Kroll, *op. cit.*, pp. xiv–xv ; U. Wilcken, *Alexander der Grosse*, Leip-sic, 1931, p. 304 ; R. M. Rattenbury, *op. cit.*, pp. 220–22 ; W. W. Tarn, *The Cambridge Ancient History*, vol. VI, Cambridge, 1927, p. 352.

make very little account of the other parts of the body, so I must be permitted to devote myself rather to the signs of the soul in men, and by means of these to portray the life of each, leaving to others the description of their great contests." [14]

Pseudo-Callisthenes might have written these words as a preface to his *Historia*.

The History of Alexander The Great
by Pseudo-Callisthenes [15]

The very learned Egyptians, who studied the size of the earth, the waves of the sea, the river Nile, the stars in heaven, bequeathed to the world the art of magic. For their first King Nectanebus ruled by that power. And when war threatened, he would take a brazen cauldron, fill it with rain water, launch a fleet of tiny boats on it, stir the water with an ebony rod, and call upon the messengers and the Libyan god Ammon.

Now once an informer brought in a report that many barbarian tribes were rising against the King. He resorted to his cauldron only to find to his horror that the gods of the Egyptians were piloting the ships of his enemies and that he had been betrayed. At once disguising himself by shaving his head and beard and taking all the gold he could, he fled from Egypt and finally came to Macedonia to Pella. Here he posed as an astrologer. The Egyptians, on consulting an oracle about the disappearance of their ruler, were told that their old King had fled from Egypt, but after a time would reappear as a young man, having encircled the world and conquered his enemies.

---

[14] *Plutarch's Lives, Alexander*, vol. VII, New York, 1919, translated by B. Perrin, in *The Loeb Classical Library*, p. 225.

[15] This narrative is based on the Greek text of *Historia Alexandri Magni* (Pseudo-Callisthenes), vol. I, W. Kroll, Berlin, 1926.

Meanwhile in Macedonia the fame of the astrologer
spread so that Queen Olympias (her husband Philip was
away at war) summoned him to her palace. Her beauty
stirred desire in the heart of Nectanebus. When she
questioned him about his art, he assured the Queen that
he was a magician and an astrologer, and then proceeded
to illustrate his powers. Arranging all the paraphernalia
of magic (his tablet of bronze and ivory, of gold and silver,
with its three zones, his magic chain with the seven stars,
the sun, and the moon) he asked the Queen what she
desired to learn. "I wish to know about my relations to
Philip," she answered. "For rumor says that after the
war he will discard me and marry another." Nectanebus
assured her that this idle talk was false. "But," he added,
"in time to come you will need my aid. For it is fated
that you consort with a god and conceive a child and the
time is at hand. Tonight in a dream he will appear to
you, the horns of Ammon on his gray head."

That night by his magic Nectanebus sent to the Queen
a dream of the god and his embrace. Awakening she
wished only to make the dream reality. So she summoned
her magician and begged to be allowed to meet the god
in her waking hours. Nectanebus promised, if she would
give him a bedroom in her palace, to contrive this favor.
So in the night through his magic, he appeared to her first
as a serpent, then as the horned Ammon, then as Heracles,
then as Dionysus. But finally in his own form he embraced her. Then arising and smiting her body he cried :
"The child you have conceived will be free and uncon-
querable."

Later when Olympias was in terror over Philip's vengeance upon his return on finding her with child, Nectanebus sent to the King a dream-vision of Ammon consort-
ing with his wife and the King's soothsayers interpreted

the dream to mean that she was to bear a child to the god. Now though Philip accepted this interpretation of his dream, suspicions of a human lover began to arise in his mind. Hence Nectanebus again employing magic, when the court was banqueting, took on the likeness of a serpent and creeping to the Queen's couch touched her lips with his forked tongue and having proved his adoration vanished. Philip and the court recognized this manifestation of the divine lover and the King rejoiced that he would be called the father of a divine child.

There were also other omens. Once when Philip was sitting in the garden a bird flew to his bosom and laid an egg there, which rolled to the ground and broke. A tiny serpent issued from it and, encircling the egg from which it came, it tried to reenter it, but died before it could. The soothsayer Antiphon interpreted the omen to the King saying : "You shall have a son who shall be king and travel over the whole world subduing all men. But after a little time, turning back to his own country, he shall die."

In the fullness of time Olympias came to the hour of child-bearing. Nectanebus stood beside her chair and bade her rise a little and delay delivery until the propitious star of Hermes rose that she might bear a son who should be a scholar, a warrior, a man of many ideas. When the proper hour came and the child was born, lightning flashed, thunder sounded, earth quaked. Philip ordered this son of a god to be reared and named Alexander. All Pella, all Thrace and Macedon rejoiced.

As the boy grew up, he did not resemble Philip or Olympias. He had hair like a lion's mane. His eyes were different in color, one white, one black. His teeth were sharp as a basilisk's, his nature as passionate as a wild lion's. Many teachers the lad had and Aristotle taught him philosophy. And after a time as he was being educated the boy began to think of ruling and he would train his school-mates in battle. Certain rulers of Cappadocia brought Philip as a gift a huge wild foal that ate men. Philip accepted it and shut it up intending to use it as an executioner of lawless criminals.

When he was twelve, Alexander in full armor visited the troops with his father and joined in the manoeuvres so that the King exclaimed : "Child, I love your disposition, but I hate your appearance, for you are unlike me in looks, but like me in nature." Once when Philip was away, Olympias summoned Nectanebus to inquire what Philip intended in regard to her. As Nectanebus was consulting the stars on his tablet, Alexander asked him whether he could really see these stars in the sky and Nectanebus answered : "Yes, at night." So at night the astrologer took the lad out to view the heavens. But for all his astrology and magic Nectanebus did not see his own fate approaching. For while he was pointing out the stars to Alexander, the youth lifted him on his shoulders and hurled him on the earth. "Why, my child, did you do this ?" cried the smitten man. "Blame yourself, astrologer," retorted the youth, "for, not understanding earthly matters, you seek to know heavenly." "I am dying, Alexander," said Nectanebus. "And no mortal can conquer his fate. I knew that I must one day die at the hand of my son and now you have killed me." Then Nectanebus revealed how he had lain with Olympias in the guise of the god Ammon and he breathed his last. Alexander, wasting no time in regret, only said to the dead man : "You have paid for your deception of Philip and Olympias. I suffer, father, for what my hand has done, but I am guiltless."

Then lifting the body on his shoulders he bore it to the palace to his mother. And he told her all Nectanebus' story. And the Queen, though she had been bewitched by magic and betrayed, yet gave Nectanebus fitting burial. Philip on returning to his palace sent a mission to Delphi to learn from the oracle who should be king after him and conquer all nations. The oracle said it would be the one who should subdue the wild horse Bucephalus and drive it through Pella. Philip now began to look for some young Heracles.

Alexander and other young princes studied with the sophist Aristotle. Alexander was loved by all, for he was passionate and warlike, but Aristotle admired his mind. Now when Alexander was fourteen years old, going through the city he came to where the horse Bucephalus was confined and hearing his loud roaring inquired about him and learned his story. When Alexander approached his stall, suddenly the horse neighed gently as if ordered by some god, extended his feet and tried to make obeisance as to a master. Alexander had the stall opened and grasping his mane mounted and rode Bucephalus without a bridle. Philip on hearing the news, remembering the oracle, greeted his son as ruler of the world.

When Alexander was fifteen, he persuaded Philip to let him go to Pisa to contend in the chariot-race, for he had been training horses of his own against that day. Philip gave his consent. Alexander's friend Hephaestion went with him. And on the Pisan plain in spite of the taunts of rival princes Alexander won the prize in the chariot-race, a crown of wild-olive.

When the prince returned to Pella, he found that King Philip had put aside Olympias and taken a new wife, Cleopatra, the sister of Attalus, and was celebrating their nuptials. Alexander presented his victor's crown to his father and announced: "Father, when I shall give my mother in marriage, I will invite you to my mother's wedding." Philip was terrified, but a wit present named Lysias told the King not to be disturbed, for his new bride was so young that she would soon bear him fine sons who would be legitimate and resemble their father. Alexander in rage hurled a cylix at Lysias and killed him. Philip drawing his sword rushed at his own son, but stumbled and fell. Alexander disarming him, exclaimed : "Philip, who was hastening to capture Asia and overthrow Europe, could not cross his own floor !" After a few days, Alexander, by his persuasive words first to Philip, then to Olympias, brought his father and mother together again.

And now Alexander became busy with other matters. Cities which had revolted from Philip, refusing to pay tribute, he visited and won back, not by force of arms, but by persuasion. When ambassadors from Darius came to demand tribute from Philip, it was the prince who sent them back with the haughty message : "Tell Darius : when Philip was alone, he paid tribute to you. Now that he has a son Alexander, he no longer pays it. But that which you took from him, I arriving in person will presently take back."

Now a great and wealthy Thessalonian, Pausanias, fell in love with Queen Olympias and, when she refused his written appeals, he found an occasion for violence. Selecting a time when Alexander was absent in a war and Philip was attending certain games, he appeared beside Philip fully armed, smote him through the ribs with a spear and in the uproar hastened to the palace to kidnap the Queen. Philip was still alive, but in agony. He kept calling for Alexander and bequeathing to him the duty of vengeance. At dawn Alexander returned. Learning what had happened, he marched with his bodyguard to the palace, seized Pausanias in his mother's room and dragged him bound to his father. Philip was no longer able to speak, but when Alexander handed him his sword, he mustered his force and stabbed his foe. After that he found voice to say farewell : "My son Alexander, it is fated that you will rule the world. Remember your father Philip. My day is done." Alexander gave him splendid burial and over his grave erected a temple. The presence of Alexander comforted Olympias and the Macedonians.

Soon Alexander began to prepare for an expedition against the barbarians. He received and armed all the young volunteers. He persuaded the old veterans of his father's armies to accompany him to give courage and counsel to the troops. A large and mixed army he mustered and he assembled triremes also. Then he proceeded from Macedonia to Thrace, then to Lycaonia, then to Sicily. There Roman generals sent him a gold crown, soldiers, and money. He then went to Africa, secured Libya and visited the shrine of Ammon. And worshipping Ammon he begged to know whether that god was his real father. Ammon confirmed his divine parentage by a dream and in an oracle bade him secure eternal fame by building a city above the Island of Proteus where a great god was ruling. By travel and investigation Alexander ascertained that the spot indicated by the oracle was at the mouth of the Nile. There after careful planning and with the help of many architects he built Alexandria. No other city was greater, not Syrian Antioch nor African Carchedon nor Babylon nor Rome. He built too the great altar there and he sacrificed upon it and begged the god of the place to reveal himself to him. It was Serapis who answered his prayer, appearing in his dreams, and Serapis assured him that the name of his city Alexandria should last forever. Then Alexander begged the god to reveal when he should die, but the day of doom, he was told, no mortal may learn : he was fated to traverse many lands and conquer many people ; finally the city which he had founded would be his monument. Alexander then built a great altar to Serapis, offered sacrifices to him and went on his way.[16]

Taking his army he went to Egypt, sending the Liburnian ships to await him at Tripolis. The army became weary, for the journey was very hard. The prophets in each city greeted him as the young Sesonchosis, the ruler of the world. In Memphis they set him on the throne of Hephaestus and robed him as an Egyptian king. Now Alexander saw a statue of black stone with an inscription on its base : "The King who fled will come back to Egypt, not in old age, but young, and he will subdue our enemies the Persians." On inquiry Alexander learned that this was Nectanebus and acclaimed him as his father. And he asked the people for tribute that he might provision the city of Alexandria and they gladly gave it.

Then he marched on into Syria. He subdued the nearest cities, but Tyre refused entrance to him because an oracle had said : "If a king passes through you, your city will be utterly destroyed." Alexander sent them a letter offering peaceful relations, but promising to fulfill the oracle if they should not receive him. The Tyrians only crucified his messengers. Then Alexander besieged the city, sacked it, and levelled it to the ground.

At this time King Darius sent an embassy to Alexander

[16] The site of the Serapeum at Alexandria has now been proved beyond question to have been on the rock crowned by the so-called "Pompey's Pillar." The founder and date of the first edifice are uncertain. It was Ptolemy III who built here the first great Graeco-Egyptian Temple of Serapis. The site of the Tomb of Alexander has not yet been identified. See articles on "The Serapeum at Alexandria" and "The Tomb of Alexander" by A. J. B. Wace, to be published in the *Bulletin of the Faculty of Arts* of the University of Alexandria, vol. II.

bearing a letter, a whip, a ball, and gold. The letter bade him, since he was a mere lad, go back to his mother to be disciplined and play ball with his fellows ; and it said that gold was furnished so that he could transport his army home, but if he did not depart, he and his followers would be captured and crucified. Alexander's armies were terrified at the message, but Alexander told them it was only the barking of a frightened dog. He entertained the ambassadors, rejected a proposal that one of them made to betray Darius, and finally sent them home with a letter to the King. With irony he answered all Darius' insults, telling him he would keep the whip to lash the Persians, when they were conquered, and the ball as a symbol of the whole world that he was to rule, and the gold as a token of the future tribute that Darius must render to him.

When he had dismissed the ambassadors, he marched into Asia. Meanwhile Darius on receiving Alexander's letter communicated with his satraps, ordering them to take Alexander and send him alive to himself that he might return the young upstart to his mother's care. The satraps replied that they were powerless and implored Darius' aid. Darius answered that they were a disgrace to his kingdom since they feared such a marauder. And he proceeded to write another threatening epistle to Alexander bidding him come to render him obeisance. Alexander's only answer was to carry the war on through Arabia. A great battle followed in which the Persians hoped to conquer by their scythe-bearing chariots, but Alexander's strategy won the day. The battle was, however, a terrible one in its confusion and slaughter before the Persians were routed. Amyntas and his forces fled to Darius, and Darius under cover of night left his chariot, which was conspicuous, and escaped on horseback. Alex-

ander captured only the King's chariot, his weapons, his
mother, wife, and children.   Alexander passed that night
in Darius' tent.   He treated the royal women with honor
and his captives with kindness.

Darius now began to muster far greater forces.   Alexander learning of these preparations went over to Achaia.
He visited the Pierian city of Bebrycia where a statue of
Orpheus gave him good omens.   He went into Phrygia
and at Ilium he sacrificed to Hector, Achilles, and the
other heroes.   And when he saw how small the Scaman-
der river was and that the shield of Ajax made of seven
ox-hides was not very large, he exclaimed : "How fortunate you were in having such a herald as Homer !   For
in his poems you are great, but in reality you do not deserve what he wrote of you."

Past Abdera he journeyed, on to Bottia and Olynthus,
and he took all the land of the Chalcidians and proceeded
to the Euxine Sea and took all the cities there.   The journey onward was full of hardships : for food they even had
to kill the horses and eat their flesh.   But Alexander
cheered his men by a speech and a god encouraged them,
for Apollo of the Acragantini greeted him as Heracles
Alexander and his priestess said this meant that Alexander
would be stronger than all men and be remembered forever.

When Alexander came to Thebes, the citizens shut
their gates and sent a message by a band of soldiers that
he was to fight or depart from the city.   With a smile
Alexander replied : "I will fight against you as cowards,
shut within your walls.   Already I have made you slaves.
Brave men fight in the open plain ; women shut themselves up."   Then the awful siege of Thebes began and
within three days the walls were breached, the city set
on fire, the inhabitants massacred.

While the siege was going on, a Theban named Ismenias, a minstrel and a wise man, grieving for his city and for the young men perishing, took his pipes and made a song if haply it might move Alexander to pity. With tears streaming down his face, first he begged Alexander to spare the city that had been the nurse of Dionysus and Heracles, his forefathers, and then he sang his song. In it were celebrated the building of Thebes, all its myths, its monuments. And once again the bard craved pity in the name of Thebes' glory and her gods. But Alexander answered savagely in another song, denouncing the poet and his appeal. So as the walls of Thebes rose to the music of Amphion's lyre, now Thebes was destroyed to the accompaniment of Ismenias' dirge. And the Thebans perished with their city. But a few escaping sent to Delphi an inquiry as to whether they should ever rebuild Thebes. The oracle replied that Hermes, Alcides and Polydeuces who fights with the cestus having contended for prizes should rebuild Thebes.

Alexander went on to Corinth, was welcomed there and presided at the Isthmian games. As he crowned the victors, he saw one man Cleitomachus who was a remarkable athlete. When he came to be crowned for his javelin-hurling, Alexander said : "If you win the other two victories, I will grant you any favor you ask." When Cleitomachus won also in boxing and in the pancration, and came for his three crowns, the herald asked from what city he came. He said he had no city. And when Alexander expressed surprise, the victor said : "I had a city before Alexander was king, but since he became king, I lost my country." Then Alexander knowing what he meant and what favor he would ask, quickly exclaimed : "Let Thebes be rebuilt in honor of the three gods, Hermes, Heracles and Polydeuces ; let this be my free gift to you, not the promised answer to your prayer." So the oracle of Apollo was fulfilled.

Alexander went from Corinth to Plataea where a priestess did him honor, but the Plataean general Stasagoras who offended him was removed from office. Fleeing to Athens he stirred up the city against Alexander. A sharp correspondence between Alexander and Athens ensued, for the city refused to pay him annual tribute. And when Alexander asked them to send him their ten leading orators to discuss matters, they deliberated. In the assembly which the Athenians held, Aeschines advised them to send the orators, for Alexander, the pupil of Aristotle, would surely respect them and be influenced by their words. Demades in answer recalling the Athenian victories over the Persians advised uncompromising war. Demosthenes, however, argued that Xerxes the barbarian was a very different foe from Alexander the Greek ; that Athens was in no position to resist the young victor, but should court his friendship. Demosthenes' advice prevailed and the Athenians sent to Alexander at Plataea a victor's crown and friendly greetings. They did not send the orators. Alexander replied with a long explanatory letter :

"I, Alexander, son of Philip and my mother Olympias — for I will not call myself king until I have subjected all the barbarians to the Greeks — sent for your ten orators not to injure them, but to use them as counsellors and that I might approach Athens, not with an army, but with your orators. So you mistrusted my father. And I might wish to punish you were I too not an Athenian. But you have treated your own citizens as unjustly as you did Philip : Eucleides, Demosthenes, Alcibiades, Socrates, the teacher of Hellas. . . I have heard of the speeches of Aeschines, Demades and Demosthenes in your assembly and what they advised. However you shall go on being Athenians and you shall receive no harm from me. For I think it unfitting when I am fighting against the barbarians in behalf of freedom to destroy Athens the seat of freedom."

He proceeded with his army to the Lacedaemonians. They closed their gates and manned their ships. A warning letter did not alter their resolve to fight, but when Alexander's army destroyed the defenders of the walls and fired the ships, the survivors came as suppliants, begging not to be taken captive. Alexander rebuked them for their folly in thinking that because they had driven out Xerxes, they could resist Alexander, but he left them their bereft city and went on his way to the land of the barbarians through Cilicia. Darius alarmed at his approach thought of giving up Greece that he might rule his own people, but his brother Oxyathres told him instead to prepare for war and to imitate Alexander in leading his own forces on the field of battle.

In his journey through Cilicia Alexander because he bathed in a cold river became violently ill. A physician named Philip was preparing a medicinal draught to relieve him, when a letter was given to Alexander from his general Parmenion saying that Philip had been persuaded by Darius to poison Alexander by the promise of marriage to Darius' daughter and a share in the kingdom. Alexander put the letter under his pillow, looked straight at Philip when he entered, and drank his medicine. Then he gave the doctor the letter to read. Philip told him that Parmenion himself had proposed the poisoning and on investigation the King found this was true and executed the general. Then he marched through Media and Armenia and came to the Euphrates river. This he quickly bridged and, when the army feared to cross thinking the strong current would sweep away his structure, with his body-guard he led them over. Then he destroyed the bridge and told the soldiers he had done it because they must either conquer and then return, or perish. So they took courage and made a camp.

The forces of Darius were encamped near the Tigris river. Five satraps led them and soon they engaged in battle. A Persian soldier, escaping the notice of the Macedonians, crept up behind Alexander and smote him on the head. Apprehended and questioned, he said that Darius had promised, if he cut off Alexander's head, to give him royal lands and his daughter. In the presence of the whole army, Alexander dismissed him as a brave soldier. Presently one of the Persian satraps came to Alexander and promised that if he would give him one thousand soldiers, he would betray to him the Persian army and Darius himself. Alexander's reply was : "Depart and help your own King. For I do not trust you with the soldiers of another when you propose to betray your own."

Now much correspondence went on : appeals of satraps to Darius ; threats of Darius to Alexander ; Alexander's cool reply and his orders to the satraps of the lands he had conquered to send him aid ; Darius' appeal to Porus, King of India, for help ; and finally a letter from Darius' mother to her son, telling him how kindly she had been treated by Alexander and urging him to come to terms with the Macedonian. At this last letter Darius wept, but proceeded on the way to war.

Alexander now purposed to send a message to Darius, but in a dream he was warned by the god Ammon to go as his own messenger, disguised as the god. Alexander following this advice was taken into the city of Persis as a holy visitant. Darius on hearing he was a messenger from Alexander made a banquet for him. During the feast a Persian who had been on an embassy to Pella recognizing Alexander revealed his identity to the King. In the uproar that followed Alexander escaped, killed a mounted guard, seized his torch and was off on his horse in the dark. He reached the Strangus river which he had crossed on the ice, but now it was a great open stream. He forded it on the horse, but on the other side the beast lost its footing and was borne away by the current. Alexander got to land, found friends waiting for him and joined his own men. He reviewed his troops and addressed them. He told them that they were greatly outnumbered by the Persians, but in courage each one was equal to a hundred of the enemy, and when wasps attack flies, the number of the flies counts as nothing.

But Darius despising Alexander's army because of its small size crossed the Strangus river and engaged the enemy in battle. Fierce was the fighting, but the Greeks routed the Persians and Darius had to turn and flee back across the river. He crossed it safely, but then the stream rose and overwhelmed his army. Back in his palace the King threw himself on his bed and wept, lamenting the overthrow that Fortune had dealt him. Then he sent a letter to Alexander begging pity from the conqueror, and promising that if Alexander would return his mother, wife, and children, he might take all the treasures of the east and all the nations of the east would acknowledge him as their lord. When Alexander called an assembly to consider this letter, Parmenion advised him to accept Darius' offer. But Alexander said he would never have made the expedition into Asia if he had not believed that the country belonged to the Greeks and only when he had conquered would he make terms with Darius.

He admired the rich tombs of the Persians with their great treasures especially the sarcophagus of Cyrus with his mummy visible through the crystal cover. Now he found mutilated Greek captives in fetters and wept over their lot. To each he gave a goodly sum of money and proposed to send them all home, but they begged to be allowed to stay there since they would be a disgrace to those at home. So he gave them plots of land, seed, cattle, and more money to start them as farmers.

Darius, meanwhile, wrote a letter to Porus telling him of his plight and begging Porus to assemble an army for him at the Caspian Gates, promising good pay for the soldiers and great rewards for himself. Alexander learned these facts from deserters and started on the trail of the King. Two satraps of Alexander, Bessus and Ariobarzanes, planned to kill Darius, expecting a reward from Alexander. They stabbed the King and left him wounded in his palace. There Alexander found him dying and chanted a dirge of pity over him. The great King rallied and in another poem warned Alexander not to be sure of the future but to remember Tyche's power. He begged for honorable burial and pity for his wife. Also he asked Alexander to marry his daughter Roxane that if the dead have knowledge, two parents might rejoice in their children, Philip in Alexander, Darius in Roxane. Alexander gave the King royal burial and acted as one of his pall-bearers. Macedonians and Persians united in doing Darius honor.

Alexander then issued a proclamation to the Persians giving orders for the preservation of their political organization under the satraps ; the maintenance of their traditional festivals ; and the opening of the roads for free travel between Greece and Persia. Then he announced also that if the slayers of Darius, his enemy, should present themselves, they would receive a just reward. When Bessus and Ariobarzanes appeared, he had them executed.

Now he wrote a letter to Statira and Rhodogoune, telling them the facts of Darius' death, and the King's directions to himself. He assured them they should rule over whatever lands they wished ; he announced that he intended to marry Roxane and they were to reverence her as a queen. Statira and Rhodogoune replied thanking him for his mercy, accepting Roxane as queen and declaring that they had informed all Persia that he was their benefactor and ruler, and was to be worshipped as a god. Alexander answered briefly, refusing divine honors. Then he wrote to his mother Olympias and also to Roxane. He bade Roxane to reverence Nemesis and Justice and to bear no resentments, for men and gods must yield to Fortune. "Try to think thoughts worthy of Alexander," he wrote, "and to show respect to Olympias. Then you and I will live in harmony." Then after sacrifice to the gods, having heard that Porus had been preparing to fight on Darius' side, he set out for India.

The march was long, through desert land without water, and the army grew weary. Their officers began to propose going home and said if Alexander still longed for contest, let him fight alone. Falling on the ground, they showed their shattered weapons, their ragged clothing, and they counted over the brothers, sons, and fathers they had lost in twelve years of campaigning. Alexander made a speech reminding them that it was his leadership that had brought them to victory against the vast hordes of the Persians ; that he always led the van in battle ; that he had gone alone to the court of Darius and then he had warded off dangers from them. How could they return alone to Macedonia without the leadership of the King ? On hearing his speech, all begged him to forgive them and to keep them as his allies until the end.

Alexander now received an insulting letter from Porus, announcing that he was king of men and of gods ; that Alexander must depart from India at once and give up all desire of ruling what he could not possess. Alexander told his army to be no more afraid of this braggart than they had been of Darius. Alexander replied that he came to fight with Porus as a mortal, not a god, and as a mortal who was a boaster and a barbarian. Now Porus prepared a mighty host and many elephants for battle ; and the Macedonians drawing near were not afraid of the numbers, but of the wild beasts. Alexander had to invent a new weapon for fighting against them. He collected bronze statues, had them heated and carried with smoking fires inside to the front of the battle. At the first encounter the elephants who were in the Persian van charged against the statues, were badly burned and completely routed. The battle, however, continued and in it Porus captured Bucephalus. Alexander's army was so weary that it was ready to surrender. To save it he challenged Porus to single combat; his enemy accepted ; and in their duel Alexander killed the Indian King. Then he sent the Indian soldiers to their homes, gave Porus honorable burial and marched on his way.

He came to a place called Aorne because no birds flew over it. It was a height so impregnable that neither Dionysus nor Heracles had been able to capture it. Alexander had iron pegs driven in the cliff so that on them the Macedonians made the ascent and captured the rock. Alexander's courage was manifested in his storming another Indian city. When the ladders were placed against the walls, all those of the other Macedonians were broken down so they could not enter, but the ladder of Alexander held and by it the King and two friends, Peucestes and Ptolemy, entered the city and fought there against all the defenders. Alexander was finally wounded under the breast. The Macedonians perceiving what had happened broke down the gates and killed all in the city, not sparing women or children, in vengeance for their King.

The next journey was to Oxydracae, not to make war, but to visit the Brahman Gymnosophists.   Of them he asked many questions, but they in return asked only one favor of him, immortality.   And when he said he too was mortal and could not confer that boon, they asked why then he kept making wars when what he won, he could not carry away with him.   Alexander could answer only that some divine providence like the wind on the sea and the trees drove him on.

Thereafter Alexander wrote a long letter to Aristotle, recounting the marvels they had seen and the deeds they had done : a disappearing island ; an eclipse of the sun and the moon ; the victory over the Persians ; an island city built on reeds ; a spring of sweet water to which all manner of marvellous beasts came to drink ; a sacred grove where two trees named the Sun and the Moon gave vocal oracles.   From them Alexander told Aristotle he received a message that he would be killed by his own people, would die in Babylon and not be taken back to his mother Olympias, and after a little time his mother, his wife, and his sisters would be killed by his people.

Such was the letter of Alexander to Aristotle.   Then he led his army to the city of Semiramis.   The ruler there was a very beautiful woman named Candace, a descendant of Semiramis.   Alexander wrote a letter to this Queen saying he had heard in Egypt that once she ruled that country and that Ammon had made an expedition with her ; he begged her now to come to the border of her country, bringing the shrine and statue of Ammon that he might sacrifice to the god ; and if she did not wish to come with it, he hoped to meet her soon in Meroe for consultation.

Candace replied that once Ammon had made an ex-

pedition with her, but now it was not lawful that he should
leave the country or that any one should enter it ; Alexander must not suppose her people dark-skinned : they
were whiter than any in his army ; he would do well to
sacrifice to Ammon ; she had prepared great gifts for him,
gold, a crown for Ammon, elephants and other wild beasts,
ivory, ebony ; he should send an embassy to receive these
presents ; and when he had conquered the world, he must
write to her.   Alexander sent Cleomenes to receive the
Queen's gifts and when Candace learned from him all the
prowess of Alexander, she sent back with Cleomenes one
of her artists to paint for her a portrait of Alexander.
And having received it she hid it in a secret place.

Now the son of Candace, Candaules, with a few horse-
men went to the tent of Alexander.   As the King was
asleep, Ptolemy Soter received him and asked his business.
Candaules said his wife had been carried off by the tyrant
of the Bebrycians and he wished aid for vengeance.   When
Ptolemy reported this to Alexander, the King bade him
return to Candaules wearing his crown and cloak, to im-
personate Alexander and to summon himself as Antigonus.   This Ptolemy did and when as King Alexander he
asked advice from the pseudo-Antigonus about Candaules' request, "Antigonus" asked to be sent with Candaules to assist his expedition.   When they attacked the
city of the Bebrycians, the people rose against their tyrant,
slew him and gave Candaules back his wife.   Candaules
in joy begged "Antigonus" to return home with him to
his mother to receive royal gifts.   Ptolemy gave permission to "Antigonus" to go, but demanded from Candaules
a promise of his safe return.

They travelled through a land full of wonders : mountains towering to the clouds, trees bearing golden apples
with great dragons guarding them and sacred to the gods.

When they came to the palace, Candaules' mother and brothers met them, and before Candaules embraced them he made them welcome his guest and savior. Then he told them of their expedition. That night there was a banquet at which Candace appeared in her royal garb looking so beautiful that "Antigonus" marvelled not only at the works of art in the palace, but at the Queen. Indeed he thought he saw his own mother Olympias before him. Candace led him to her bed-chamber and suddenly when they were alone, addressed him as Alexander. "Look," she said, "do you not recognize your portrait here? Why do you tremble? Why are you dismayed? The conqueror of the Persians and the Indians, the one who took trophies from Medes and Parthians, now without a war or an expedition has fallen into the hands of Queen Candace. Know, Alexander, that whoever prides himself on his intelligence, will meet another with a brain greater than his own." Alexander, raging, replied : "If I had my sword, I would kill you first, then myself." Candace then assured him that she would protect him as Antigonus, for if her people knew he was Alexander, they would kill him because he killed Porus, since the wife of her youngest son was a daughter of Porus. And, indeed, her youngest son made a strong plea that they should kill this Antigonus to vex Alexander, but he was overruled.

So Alexander was sent home with many gifts and on his journey he stopped at one of the holy caves, entered and offered sacrifice. There he saw images with fiery light gleaming from their eyes and one, who said he was Sesonchosis, prophesied to him that the city he was building would be immortal ; there many kings should do obeisance to him ; and the city would be his burial-place. Then Alexander went on his way.

He came to the country of the Amazons and wrote a letter to them, asking for a meeting, since he had arrived to see their country and be their benefactor.   Their answer described to him their island home and informed him that they were maiden warriors ; the men of the country lived across the river and were farmers ; once a year the Amazons who wished consorted with them and any girls who were born, when they were seven years old, joined the Amazons ; if any enemy attacked them, they fought on horseback and there were prizes for prowess. They requested an answer from Alexander about his intentions.   He replied that since he had conquered three parts of the world, he could not pass them by.   He swore that if they would cross the river and have the men assemble in the plain, he would do them no harm ; they should state what tribute they would pay and he would not enter their land ; he asked hostages from them who should remain a year and then return to their home while others took their places.   The Amazons acceded to these terms adding the stipulation that, if any Amazon consorted with a foreigner, she should not return to their island.

Then Alexander marched into the Prasiacan land, a terrible journey, for there were forty days of rain, followed by intense heat and thunder-storms.   A great enemy too was mustered in the Prasiacan land.   So Alexander simply ravaged the country along the Hypanis river without crossing it and set up altars on which sacrifices were offered to the gods.

Alexander received a letter from Aristotle congratulating him on his mighty conquests.   Going on to Babylon, he was greatly honored there and celebrated athletic games and a musical contest.   He now wrote to his mother Olympias an account of his exploits and his travels : to the pillars of Heracles, to the Thermodon river and the

Amazons ; to the Red Sea and the river Atlas near which
live dog-headed men and men without heads with eyes
and mouth in their chests ; to the city of Heliopolis ; to
the Tanais river ; to the palace of Cyrus and Xerxes and
to Susa, where is the wondrous throne.

After that when he was in Babylon and about to leave
this life, a terrible omen was revealed to him.   A woman
brought to him a monstrous child that she had borne,
above the waist a boy, but below a dreadful Scylla composed of parts of wild animals.   Alexander summoned
the wizards and the Chaldeans to interpret the omen but
only one Chaldean had the courage to tell him the truth :
that his days were numbered, for evil creatures were
crowding around the little of his life that remained.   The
Chaldean ordered that the child should be burned and
Alexander prayed to Zeus to lead him to the end and
finally to receive him to heaven as he had Dionysus and
Heracles.

Now Olympias wrote her son that Antipater was treat-
ing her contemptuously and Alexander suspecting Antipater's plans sent Craterus into Macedonia.   Antipater
was planning to kill Alexander.   He secured a poison so
strong that only the hoof of a mule could hold it and gave
this in an iron case to Casander his son to bear as a gift
to the King.   When Casander arrived in Babylon, he
got in touch with Iollas, the royal cup-bearer, for he found
Iollas was disaffected because recently he had been struck
for some misdemeanor.   At a symposium Iollas found
his chance and served the poison to Alexander in his
drink.   After a little, suddenly Alexander shrieked as if
he had been smitten in his heart by an arrow.   Mastering
the pain he withdrew ordering them to go on drinking.
Alexander asked for a feather for he used this as an
emetic.   But Iollas gave him one smeared with more of

the poison. The next day he was worse. Casander went away in the night and at the mountains of Cilicia waited for Iollas, for he had promised to come as soon as Alexander died. He sent a messenger by sea to his father to tell him in code how matters were shaping.

Alexander during the night ordered all to leave the house, among them Roxane his wife, and he directed that a certain door of the house from which a path led to the Euphrates river should be left unguarded. At midnight he rose from his bed and going out through that door walked towards the river. But the Queen Roxane suspecting his intentions came running to meet him. She embraced him as he groaned and supporting him took him back into the house.

When day came, he summoned Perdiccas, Ptolemy, Lysimachus and two secretaries that he might make his will. Perdiccas having an idea that Alexander would make Ptolemy his successor drew the unsuspecting youth apart and made him swear on oath to divide with him any powers which Alexander bequeathed him. After a day and a night Alexander summoned Perdiccas, Olcias, Ptolemy and Lysimachus. On this the Macedonians all demanded to be allowed to see their King and, when Alexander heard their uproar at the door, he gave orders that they should march by his bed. So they passed by him encouraging him and weeping at what had happened to their great King. One of them, Peucolaus, standing near Alexander spoke :

"O Alexander, Philip ruled Macedonia wisely and so did you." Then weeping and continuing in the Macedonian dialect he said : "If you leave us, Macedonia has perished." Alexander wept and clasped his hand.

When they had marched through the room, Alexander called back Perdiccas and the others and bade Olcias read his will. The superscription was : "King Alexander son of Ammon and Olympias salutes the generals, the archons, the senate, the people of the Rhodians." It first enjoined upon them the preservation of freedom for Greece. Then it set forth the following provisions. His body was to be entrusted to the Egyptian priests for burial with appropriate funds. Thebes was to be rebuilt and given food until the land could produce a livelihood. The carrying out of his directions was entrusted to Craterus, Ptolemy, Perdiccas, and Antigonus ; Ptolemy in particular was to guard his body.

For the present Arridaeus son of Philip was to be ruler of Macedonia. If Roxane should bear a son to Alexander, he should be king ; if she should bear a daughter, let the Macedonians choose their own king if they should not wish Arridaeus to rule. The one selected should rule the Argeiadae. His mother Olympias should be spared and allowed to live in Rhodes if the Rhodians consented. If they did not, let her live wherever she wished.

Until the Macedonians selected a king, the ruling power was to be distributed as follows : Macedonia to Craterus and his wife Cyane, daughter of Philip ; Thrace to Lysimachus and his wife Thessalonice, daughter of Philip ; the satrapy of the Hellespont to Leonnatus and his wife Cleodice, the sister of Olcias ; Paphlagonia and Cappadocia to Eumenes ; the islands should be free with the Rhodians as overlords ; Pamphylia and Cilicia to Antigonus ; Babylon to Seleucus; Phoenicia and Syria to Ptolemy and as wife Cleopatra, the sister of Alexander ; the land above Babylonia to Phanocrates and as wife to him Roxane of Bactria.

A golden coffin should be prepared for the body of Alexander the King. The older and weaker men of the Macedonians and Thessalians should be sent home and each given three talents of gold. The armor of Alexander and fifty talents of gold should be sent to Argos as an offering to Heracles, and to Delphi elephants' tusks, dragon spears and gold bowls. The Milesians must be given money to restore their city.

Alexander provided that Perdiccas, who was to be king of Egypt with Alexandria, should preserve the worship of Serapis and should appoint a priest of Alexander who should receive yearly a talent of gold, should wear a gold crown and purple, and be highly honored ; and these privileges should be hereditary in his family.

Alexander appointed Porus King of India and Oxydraces, father of Roxane, wife of Alexander, King over the Paropanisadae. (Other rulers were appointed for other parts of the east.) Olcias was to be King of Illyria and was to prepare a shrine with statues of Ammon, Heracles, Athena, and Olympias, wife of Philip. Perdiccas too was to set up statues of Alexander, Ammon, Heracles, Olympias. Such was Alexander's will.

Now Ptolemy approaching him asked : "Alexander, to whom do you leave your kingdom?" He replied : "To the one who is strong and purposeful, who conserves and who accomplishes." At these words darkness filled the air and a great star fell from the sky into the sea and with it a great eagle fell and the bronze statue of Zeus in Babylon was shaken. Then the star returned to the sky, the eagle with it carrying a bright star. And when the star was hidden in heaven, Alexander closed his eyes.

Then the Persians and the Macedonians contended for the honor of taking the body of Alexander to their countries. When Ptolemy consulted the oracle of Babylonian Zeus, the answer was that Alexander was to be buried in Memphis and worshipped there as the horned King. So Ptolemy with all due ceremony escorted the body to Memphis. But there the arch-priest said that Alexander's body was to rest in Alexandria, the city which he had founded. So Ptolemy buried him in Alexandria with fitting splendor.

Alexander in his wars did not conquer as many kings as dying he created. Alexander lived thirty years. He subdued twenty-two barbarian tribes, ten Greek. He founded thirteen cities, several named Alexandria. He was born in Τῦβι at the rising of the new moon and he died in Φαρμοῦθι on the fourth day at sunset.[17]

The first point that must strike any reader of this narrative is the inconsistencies in the plot. Three are glaring. Porus, the Indian King, who in III. 4 was killed by Alexander in battle, in the will of Alexander is ordered to rule over India. Roxane, who in II. 20 ff., is said to be the daughter of Darius, in the will is referred to twice, as the daughter of Oxydraces, which she was, and as a Bactrian. And third, although in his will Alexander had given directions about his successor and his place of burial, in the following narrative both points are taken up as new subjects. Since all of these inconsistencies occur in the will, we must conclude that this document was inserted in the completed narrative at a later date. It can hardly then be considered as a part of the Alexander Romance.[18]

Similar inconsistencies have been pointed out by Ausfeld in the many letters which form an important part of the narrative. To illustrate, in the letter of Alexander to the Tyrians, Alexander is called the great King of Asia although he had not yet subdued Asia.[19] In the letter

---

[17] Τῦβι is the Egyptian equivalent of the Macedonian Δύστριος, = Dec. 27–Jan. 25 ; Φαρμοῦθι is the Egyptian equivalent of the Macedonian Δαίσιος, March 27–April 25. G. Milligan, *Selections from the Greek Papyri*, Cambridge, 1910, p. xviii.

[18] W. Kroll, *op. cit.*, p. xiv; A. Ausfeld, *op. cit.*, pp. 214–15.

[19] I. 35, A. Ausfeld, *op. cit.*, p. 143.

to Olympias, the narrative about the Amazons is different
from the one given in III. 25 f.   Moreover a visit to Susa
and Persepolis is described as though he were seeing for
the first time the marvels of these cities, yet II. 17 f. had
already told of his first entrance into the Persian cities and
the burning of the royal palace.[20]   Ausfeld has pointed
out meticulously all such inconsistencies in the text and
has endeavored by eliminating them to reconstruct the
original kernel of the romance, which he proceeds to date
in the time of Ptolemy Epiphanes.[21]   Many scholars, who
do not accept his dating, profit by his "Historischer Kom-
mentar," and by his comparison of the Pseudo-Callisthenes
with the accounts of Alexander in Arrian, Diodorus, Jus-
tin, Curtius and Plutarch.

A few words must be said about the historicity of the
whole *Historia*.   It begins with a rationalized myth which
suggests an Egyptian origin for this Pseudo-Callisthenes
version.   Alexander, the reputed son of a god, the son
of Ammon, is proved to be actually the son of the last
King of Egypt Nectanebus, who came incognito to Pella
and in Philip's absence by his art of magic made love to
Olympias and embraced her, disguised first as a serpent,
then as the horned god.   Added to this remarkably circumstantial account of Alexander's parentage are the phe-
nomena of his childhood : his brilliancy in personality
and mind, his taming of Bucephalus, his moral rebukes to
his father, his intelligent questioning of the Persian ambassadors.

Fact and fancy are compounded in these tales of birth
and childhood, but when the narrative goes on to the
account of Alexander's expeditions, difficulties of credence
are equally great.   To be sure, the main campaigns, the

---

[20] III. 27–28, A. Ausfeld, *op. cit.*, p.
196.

[21] A. Ausfeld, *op. cit.*, "Die Zusätze
von *a* und ihre Quellen," pp. 243–48.

startling episodes, and the decisive battles are mentioned, but the order of the expeditions is changed. Geography and chronology are disregarded or confused. Important events like the destruction of Thebes, the visit to the shrine of Ammon in Libya, the founding of Alexandria, the visit to Ilium are introduced, but the visit to Greece with the destruction of Thebes is put after the battle of Issus and so is the visit to Ilium. Moreover, the visit to the Shrine of Ammon and the founding of Alexandria are placed before the siege of Tyre. The two great battles of Issus and Gaugamela are described, although they are not named, and the invasion of India is related.

Many of the anecdotes about the main events are the same as in the histories, but new ones are also introduced. Traditional episodes preserved are Alexander's illness in Cilicia, the meeting with the mutilated Greek captives, the inspection of the tomb of Cyrus, the visit to the Gymnosophists, revels at Babylon. New stories are the marriage to Roxane the daughter of Darius, and Darius' deathbed approval of it ; Alexander's visit in disguise to Darius ; Alexander's visit in disguise to Queen Candace ; and the battle with the elephants of Porus, which were routed by heated bronze statues. The Pseudo-Callisthenes narrative makes picturesque and lively reading, but it is *not* history : it is a romance presenting a hero who is semidivine and wholly victorious.[22] Let us now consider what are the characteristics and style of this romance.

The History of Alexander the Great shares with other Greek Romances the interests of adventure and religion, but not the interest of love. The marriage to Roxane

[22] On the historicity of the Pseudo-Callisthenes see Appendix I ; the map in G. Radet, *Alexandre le Grand*, Paris, 1931 ; A. Ausfeld, *Der Griechische Alexanderroman* nach des verfassers Tode herausgegeben von W. Kroll, Leipsic, 1907 ; C. A. Robinson, *The Ephemerides of Alexander's Expedition*, Providence, 1932, W. W. Tarn in *The Cambridge Ancient History*, vol. VI, University Press, Cambridge, 1927, cc. XII and XIII.

was not a love affair, but a political alliance. Hence she was made the daughter of Darius instead of a Bactrian princess to signalize Alexander's policy of amalgamating Greece and Persia after his conquest. To be sure, it was the dying Darius who proposed this union, but Alexander accepted the proposal in his compassion for the conquered and fallen monarch. When he wrote to inform Darius' mother and wife of his intentions, he offered to let them rule over whatever countries they wished, but they were to do obeisance to Roxane as the queen. He then wrote to his own mother Olympias of his plans and finally to Roxane. This epistle, interesting as it is, can hardly be called a love-letter. The only suggestion of what sort of a wife Roxane was to Alexander came at the end of his life. When in the agony caused by the poison, Alexander had ordered Roxane and all his retinue to leave the house and mustering all his strength he had slipped out on a path leading to the Euphrates river, Roxane, divining his intention to drown himself, found him and supported him back to the palace. There after the weeping Macedonians had filed by his bed and he had given final directions to his officers, he died in a way worthy of a king. Roxane had seen to it that he was not an unburied suicide.

Olympias, the mother of Alexander, seems to have been the dominating woman in his life and this fact the romance conveys. She was a beautiful woman who stirred men, Philip, Nectanebus, Pausanias. She was, as was natural from her Molossian origin, superstitious, susceptible to the influence of magic, suggestible in regard to Nectanebus' controlled apparitions of serpent and horned god. She believed that Ammon had embraced her and begotten her son until Alexander revealed to her Nectanebus' dying confession of his wiles. For all her power, she was constantly fearful of Philip's vengeance and because of his suspicions she could not hold his love. It was Alexander who brought Philip and Olympias together again after Philip had taken a new wife Cleopatra.[23] It was Alexander too who helped Philip slay Pausanias after he had given Philip his death-blow and was stealing his wife. Alexander appeared three times as the defender of his mother's honor.

In his invasion of Asia Alexander kept Olympias in his thoughts. He wrote to her about his marriage to Roxane as well as to Roxane about his mother. He wrote an account of his exploits and adventures in Asia to Olympias as well as to Aristotle. And when he received a letter from Olympias informing him of Antipater's slights, he at once despatched Cratcrus to Macedonia to look after her interests. Her passionate northern blood coursed in his veins.[24]

His relation to another great queen, Candace, might have been written as a love-story, although she was old enough to be his mother and, indeed, in her beauty reminded him of Olympias. His secret visit to her city and her discovery of his identity make good reading. But Candace having matched her wits against his sent him home safely and retained only the memory of her adroit conquest and his portrait ! Actually the historical Candaces lived after Alexander's time. One was subdued in 24 or 23 B.C. in Egypt, but regained her independence. Nero sent an expedition into Ethiopia against another. And a third is Biblical.[25]

[23] Actually, Alexander and his mother left the palace and stayed in Illyria until Demaratus of Corinth brought about a reconciliation. Attalus and Cleopatra were done away with only after Philip's death. A. Ausfeld, *op. cit.*, p. 132.

[24] For a fuller sketch of Olympias' life see Grace H. Macurdy, *Hellenistic Queens,* Baltimore, 1932, pp. 22–48.

[25] Act. Apost. 8, 26 ; A. Ausfeld, *op. cit.*, pp. 187–89.

The account of his correspondence with the Queen of
the Amazons and of her colony beside the Thermodon
river likewise contains no love romance.   It is a picturesque story of a new political alliance.   Passionate as
Alexander was in quick acts of violence, he is never in this
story represented as amorous.

In spite of that, the Alexander of Pseudo-Callisthenes
is a romantic hero, for our novel centers in his adventures
and like a new Achilles he is always victorious, to be conquered only by death.   He revels in danger, in daring
exploits, in single-handed combats.   He is generous to
friends and foes.   His sins are committed in temper and
passion and are deeply regretted.   He towers tall, almost
as a superman.

How is this figure of a romantic hero created ?   First
of all, an aura of mystery encircles his birth.   His mother
was Olympias, but was his father Philip, or an Egyptian
king, or the horned god Ammon ?   Myth and fact inter-
play in statement, conjecture, and faith.   The personal
description of him enhances the mystery : no resemblance
to Philip, those two-colored eyes, that leonine mane of
hair.   His phenomenal childhood and youth forecast his
powers : the taming of Bucephalus, his precocity in
studies, his victory in chariot-racing at Pisa, his moral
standards (in his self-justification for the death of Nectanebus ; in his reconciliation of Philip and Olympias) ;
his proud answer to the Persian ambassadors.

Perhaps it was the oracle of Ammon that set in his mind
the concept of the divine king and certainly the founding
of Alexandria which the oracle prescribed marked the
beginning of his aspiration for eternal fame for his name.
As we shall see, when we come to study the element of
religion in the romance, side by side with his military
prowess his mysticism developed.

A fine nobility in his character appears in his courtesies to the captive Persian Queen and princesses, to individual enemies who fell into his power, to his physician Philip, and to the dying Darius.   His personal courage is incontrovertible.   He led his troops in battle and was the first to cross the Euphrates.   He went disguised and alone to a banquet at Darius' palace and to the court of Queen Candace.   He engaged in single combat with King Porus and took an Indian city by his individual prowess.   He inspired his army to superhuman feats like his own and yielded to them gracefully, when human nature could stand no more and at Opis the officers mutinied against further advance into India.   The devotion of officers and men is portrayed in the last meeting when they filed through the bed-chamber of their dying lord and one whispered through his tears : "If you leave us, Macedonia has perished."   That touching scene was not to be the hero's requiem.   After Alexander's last words to Ptolemy, darkness came over the earth ; a star fell from the sky ; an eagle soared down and with the fallen star returned, carrying a new bright star to heaven.   Then Alexander closed his eyes.   His immortality was assured.

This vivid picture of Alexander is made more colorful and vital by the record of his pithy sayings, "a phrase or a jest," which Plutarch called "the signs of the soul in men." Some of these are traditional, in Arrian and in Plutarch ; others are unique in Pseudo-Callisthenes.   Here are specimens.

At the wedding banquet of Philip and Cleopatra when the fifteen-year-old Alexander had killed Lysias who had cast a slur on his legitimacy and King Philip with drawn sword rushed at his son, but stumbled and fell, Alexander disarming his father exclaimed : "Philip, who was hastening to capture Asia and overthrow Europe, could not cross his own floor." An ironic jest !

When ambassadors from Darius came to demand tribute from Philip, Alexander hurled at them a haughty message prophetic of his future career : "Tell Darius : when Philip was alone, he paid tribute to you. Now that he has a son Alexander, he no longer pays it. But that which you took from him, I, arriving in person, will presently take back."

His speeches to his army were often colored by homely metaphors. He told them not to fear Darius' threats : they were only the barking of a frightened dog. At another time he said to his troops that the Persians far outnumbered them, but in courage each Greek was equal to a hundred of the enemy, and when wasps attack flies, the number of the flies counts as nothing.

Other comments on warfare are equally self-revealing. When Thebes shut her gates against him, Alexander called the Thebans cowards, adding : "Already I have made you slaves. Brave men fight in the open plain ; women shut themselves up." Again when Athens refused to send him her ten best orators to discuss a treaty, Alexander replied magnanimously : "You shall receive no harm from me. For I think it unfitting, when I am fighting against the barbarians in behalf of freedom, to destroy Athens, the seat of freedom."

Outbursts of feeling appear in single sentences : at Achilles' mound : "How fortunate you were in having such a herald as Homer !" ; in Candace's boudoir : "If I had my sword, I would kill you first, then myself."

Most illuminating of all his recorded speeches is his reply to the Brahman Gymnosophists when they asked him why he made wars since he admitted he was mortal and so could carry nothing with him to the grave : "Some divine providence like the wind on the sea and the trees drives me on." His final words reveal his awareness of the qualities of the great leader. When Ptolemy asked to whom he bequeathed his kingdom, Alexander answered : "To the one who is strong and purposeful, who conserves and who accomplishes." Such remarks are indeed "signs of the soul."

The strange mysticism of this military leader's life appears in various ways. He was deeply influenced by oracles, dream, and omens. Delphi had told his father that his successor, who should be the conqueror of the world, would be the one who should break Bucephalus and ride him through Pella. What dreams of future glory must have passed through the fourteen-year-old prince's mind when, as he rode the great charger without a bridle, King Philip greeted him as the ruler of the world ? Later when he invaded Egypt, Alexander made the long trip to the Oasis of Siwah to ask Ammon at his shrine there whether he was his true father. Clearly, he had not accepted Nectanebus' story. The gracious god confirmed his hope and in an oracle directed the building of Alexandria to secure his son's eternal fame. Apollo too predicted his future power and glory by calling him Heracles Alexander. And after his visit to Candace, on his journey home, he entered a holy cave, offered sacrifice, looked on gods whose eyes emitted fiery light and heard one of them, Sesonchosis, prophesy that many kings would do obeisance to him and that his city, Alexandria, would be his burial-place and would last forever. So deep-rooted in his mind was Alexander's faith in himself, founded mystically on his divine origin, strengthened by oracles and visions. He liked to compare himself to Dionysus and Heracles, the benefactors of mankind. He erected many altars and on them made sacrifices to the gods and to his own divinity.

Omens played upon his superstition, for he must have heard the stories which encircled his birth : the kiss of the serpent bestowed on Olympias in the presence of the court to prove a god had lain with her ; Philip's dream of the broken egg and the little serpent which emerged from it, but could never reenter it ; the thunder, lightning and earthquake which accompanied his birth. Then there was the monster-child, boy above waist, wild beasts below, which foretold the evil foes who were struggling to shorten his life. Alexander seeing his fate approaching could only pray to Zeus to lead him to the end and receive him into heaven as he had Dionysus and Heracles. And at the end when Alexander could no longer speak, before he closed his eyes, he must have seen the falling star and the pouncing eagle which descended to take his soul, a new star, to the realms above.

The style of this historical romance is strangely heterogeneous. From its subject matter with the emphasis on adventure it might easily have been a straight epic narrative. Indeed, the influence of both the *Iliad* and the *Odyssey* are apparent. Alexander is the new Achilles, the epic hero, who engages in single combat with a great enemy, and who shows the same compassion for the dying Darius that Achilles did for the bereft Priam. The visit to the tomb of Achilles only emphasizes Alexander's sense of kinship to his model. The *Odyssey* too has its influence, for Alexander's visit to the holy cave in India seems strangely similar to Odysseus' descent to the lower world. But these resemblances to the two great Greek epics are structural rather than stylistic.

The actual language of the story is a queer combination of the conversational, the formal, and the poetic. All the first part is enlivened by short dialogues. This is the period of Alexander's marvellous childhood and youth.   Their myths and anecdotes are presented largely through conversation.   When the account of King Alexander's expeditions begins, the narrative is supported by documentation as if to give the effect of true history.   Letters, speeches, and the will (a later addition) all contribute to this aspect of historicity.   Some thirty-eight letters are directly quoted.   These include besides the famous ones to Aristotle, to Olympias, and to Roxane, correspondence between Alexander and Darius, between Alexander and various Greek states, between Darius and his satraps, between Alexander and the royal ladies of Darius' family, between Alexander and Candace, between Alexander and the Queen of the Amazons.   Most of these letters are brief, some long.   The ones already translated, from Alexander to the Athenians, from Alexander to Roxane, may serve as illustrations of the direct, simple, poignant style attributed to Alexander.   The will was undoubtedly added in later times to increase this element of documentation in the story.

The direct quotation of formal speeches is used for the same effect.   The best example is the report of the speeches of Aeschines, Demades, and Demosthenes in the assembly at Athens which deliberated on a reply to Alexander's letter requesting Athens to pay him annual tribute and to send him her ten leading orators to discuss the relation of Athens to himself.   Aeschines advised complete compliance.   Demades urged uncompromising war.   Demosthenes urged a conciliatory policy.   The assembly was influenced by Demosthenes' persuasive words and sent Alexander a victor's crown, but not the ten orators. His letter in reply shows that his espionage system was efficient, for he knew the contents of the speeches by the three orators.   Demosthenes, however, influenced Alexander also, for the King's letter, like Demosthenes' speech, was conciliatory. The quotation (or composition) of the three speeches and the letter vivify and dramatize an intense situation.

At the antipodes from this documentation of the romance by the insertion of letters, speeches, and the will, is the shift from prose to poetry. This occurs not merely in the introduction of metrical oracles.[26] In two situations of intense emotion poetry instead of prose is used to convey passionate feeling. The occasions are the destruction of Thebes, and the death of Darius.[27]

Such a mixture of prose and poetry in one work was familiar from the Menippean satire as the fragments of Varro and Petronius and the *Apocolocyntosis* of Seneca attest. Moreover, the Cynic philosophers used the choliambic meter to impart ethical instruction (*de morte, de superbia, de fortunae mobilitate*) just as Pseudo-Callisthenes uses it for ethical reflections. Our author however uses this meter also for straight epic narrative, but here too he had precedents in the Alexandrians. This meter was used too in both Greek and Latin sepulchral inscriptions down into the Third Century after Christ, a proof that it was a popular meter.[28] Pseudo-Callisthenes then was following tradition in using choliambic verses intermixed with his prose, both for narrative, for reflection, and for the expression of feeling on death. Let us study now the content and the effect of his choliambic passages.

When Thebes refused entrance to Alexander and bade the Macedonian depart or fight, he besieged the city. And when after three days the awful siege was approach-

[26] I. 30, I. 33, I. 47.
[27] On the choliambics see H. Kuhlmann, *De Ps.-Callisthenis carminibus choliambicis*, Diss. Münster, 1912.
[28] H. Kuhlmann, *op. cit.*, pp. 29–30.

ing its terrible end, Ismenias, the Theban minstrel, attempted by a song to arouse Alexander's pity and persuade him to spare the town. In impassioned choliambics he poured out his appeal in the name of all his city's past glory :

" 'O Alexander, do not destroy the city of your ancestral gods. Thebes' walls were built by Zethus and Amphion, sons of Zeus and Antiope. Cadmus built Thebes' palace, Cadmus who wed Harmonia, daughter of Ares and Aphrodite. Here lived hapless Oedipus, the slayer of his father. Here was the house of Amphitryon where Zeus consorted with Alcmene, who bore his son Heracles. Here too Zeus met Semele and by the thunderbolt Dionysus came to life. Here Heracles went mad and killed his wife Megara and their sons. Here at Thebes dwelt Teiresias, the great prophet. Ino and Ismene had stories centering here. Near here Pentheus was killed by his own mother in the frenzied rites of Dionysus. Near here Dirce's punishment was exacted. Here was the seat of the Sphinx whose riddle Oedipus solved. In this region the hapless Actaeon saw Artemis bathing, was changed to a deer and killed by his own hounds. Here was fought the dreadful civil war of the Seven against Thebes. Consider all the story of Thebes. Gaze upon the sepulchres of your forefather Heracles and your father Philip. Will you insult your ancestors, O child of Heracles and famous Bacchus ?'

"Alexander, glaring, gnashing his teeth, panting with anger, replied with another song :

" 'Accursed descendant of Cadmus, hated by the gods, disgrace of your people, do you suppose that you deceive Alexander ? If I take all your city and burn it, I will destroy you all after your country. For if you know my origin and my ancestors, why did you not proclaim these facts to the Thebans, saying, 'Since Alexander is our kinsman, let us not resist a fellow-citizen; let us give him command and be his allies since we stem from the same line.' But when you had no strength for defense and your power in battle was a disgrace, there came a change, for you could not resist Alexander in battle. And I order you, Ismenias, greatest of musicians, standing among the burning homes, to pipe a double dirge for the fall of Boeotia.'

"All was done as Alexander the Macedonian ordered. The walls of Cadmus fell, the palace of Lycus, the house of Labdacus. Only for remembrance of his education Alexander spared Pindar's tomb, for as a boy he had come to Thebes and studied the works of the Muses at the feet of the aged lyrist.[29] Ismenias piped the dirge of Thebes."

Of course no prose version can convey the impassioned quality of these choliambic lines or the effect of emotion in the halting, last foot of the scazons and the effective irregularities of the verses.[30] Poetry lifts passion to sublimity in both songs.

The same effect is attained by the use of choliambics on the death of Darius, but the feeling expressed is far different.[31]

"Now when the satraps, Bessus and Ariobarzanes, plotted to kill Darius, expecting to receive a reward from Alexander for the destruction of his foe, they approached him sword in hand. Darius cried : 'My masters, once my slaves, what wrong have I done you that you will destroy me ? Do not purpose worse deeds than Alexander. Let me cry to the house-tops [32] the inevitability of Fate. If King Alexander on coming shall find a king slain treacherously, he will avenge me. For it is not right that a king should see a king piteously betrayed.'

"For all his words the satraps stabbed him and left him lying by the Strangus river. There Alexander found Darius dying. Weeping he threw his own cloak over him and chanted for him a dirge :

" 'Rise above your fortune, Darius, and again be master of yourself. Take your diadem of the Persian world. Hold fast the greatness of your fame as monarch. I swear to you by all the gods that I say these words to you with truth and without deceit. To you alone I yield the diadem of the sceptres. For with you I partook of food at your table by your hearth when I came as a messenger of Alexander. Arise and rule the land. A king in misfortune must not grieve. Mortals share equally their final destiny. Who were the ones who stabbed you ? Speak, Darius. Name them, that you may have me as an avenger.'

"Darius, groaning, kissed Alexander's hands and said : 'Alexander, be not exalted at a ruler's glory. When you do godlike deeds, and think to hold heaven in your hands, consider the future. For Fortune knows no king nor bandit nor crowd, but she casts

---

[29] This, of course, is an anachronism. H. Kuhlmann, *op. cit.*, p. 29.

[30] H. Kuhlmann, *op. cit.*, p. 23, "Omnium igitur, quos novimus, choliamborum poetarum liberrima arte metrica utitur."

[31] II. 20.

[32] Here begin the choliambics.

forth fateful arrows on all alike. See who I was, how brave ! The lord of so great a land, now I die, not master of myself. Bury me with your reverent hands. Let Macedonians and Persians attend me. Let Darius have one family. And in my woe I entrust to you my mother and my wife, as pitiful kinswomen. My daughter Roxane I give to you in order that, if the dead have any consciousness, two fathers may rejoice in their children, Philip in you, Darius in Roxane.'

"Having spoken these words, Darius breathed his last in the arms of Alexander."

The compassion of this great scene when East meets West and the dying old King yields to the young victor is matched only by Homer. The reader's mind inevitably goes back to the scene in Achilles' hut when Priam kissed those murderous hands which had slain so many of his sons and Achilles thought of his own aged father in Phthia who would never behold his son again. Part of the art of the Alexander Romance lies in the implicit resemblances of Alexander to the Greek epic hero. And in these two passages in poetry Alexander like Achilles is shown at his worst and at his best. Alexander too must have his wrath. Alexander too must show his mercy. And only poetry can convey the depth of his emotions.

Such a man was Alexander, the hero of a Greek romance. As time went on, his figure became not merely that of "The painful warrior famoused for fight," but the prototype of all aspirants to dominion of the world. In the Roman Republic and Empire, he was a model for Julius Caesar and Augustus, for Caligula, for Nero, most of all for Trajan, for Caracalla, and for Alexander Severus. This *exemplum Alexandri* not only played a great rôle in the Roman Empire, but exerted its influence in the Eastern world. Among the Turks, Mohammed II, the sacker of Constantinople, followed in Alexander's footsteps.[33]

Through the Middle Ages and thereafter, Alexander

[33] F. Pfister, *op. cit.*, pp. 1152–59.

became par excellence the hero of adventurous warfare, and the Alexander Romance alone, in its various versions in East and West, rivalled the Achilles or Troy Romance. Through the Latin translations of Julius Valerius (at the end of the Third Century) and of the Archpresbyter Leo (Tenth Century) the Alexander Romance of Pseudo-Callisthenes became known to all Europe.   Its fame extended to the Semitic people of the East and the Coptic land to the South.[34]   As Tarn says,

"around him the whole dream-world of the East took shape and substance ; of him every old story of a divine world-conqueror was told afresh.   More than eighty versions of the Alexander-romance, in twenty-four languages, have been collected, some of them the wildest of fairy-tales ; they range from Britain to Malaya ; no other story in the world has spread like his." [35]

Glover comments :

"Now it was the Huns and now the Turks that the hero repelled. The book was done into Latin, into Armenian, into Arabic and thence into Syriac and Persian, into Hebrew from the Latin, into Turkish, into Ethiopic from the Arabic version of the Greek, and so forth." [36]

Look in the catalogue of any great library under *Alexander Romance* and see how many works are listed on the mediaeval versions in English, French, Spanish, and other languages.   Through the ages, the West united with the East in declaring : "He was of knyghthood and of fredom flour." [37]

Much remains to be done in studying the influence of the Alexander Romance.   It would be valuable to trace

[34] W. von Christ, *op. cit.*, p. 813 ; U. Wilcken, *op. cit.*, pp. 304–5 ; Ausfeld regrets that "dieses schlechte Buch" had a greater influence in the Middle Ages than any reliable history of the true Alexander. But Ausfeld pronounces his judgments on the Pseudo-Callisthenes always as if it were a history. He does not consider its effect and significance as a romance. A. Ausfeld, *op. cit.*, pp. 252–53.

[35] W. W. Tarn, *op. cit.*, p. 435.

[36] T. R. Glover, *Life and Letters in the Fourth Century,* University Press, Cambridge, 1901, p. 360.

[37] G. Chaucer, *op. cit.*, 3832.

the changing concepts of the romantic hero evolving around Alexander's name in West and East and the added adventures which each new ideal begot. In such a study it should always be remembered that in Pseudo-Callisthenes, our earliest Greek version unless we include Plutarch's *Life of Alexander* in the field of romance, the real Alexander dominates the picture. For although his psychic changes are never summarized, the Alexander of the romance is the Alexander of the historians. He is a mystic and a realist. He constructs his conception of empire on the ideas of the supremacy of the divine king and the unity of his subjects, based on the brotherhood of man. And he comes to believe that as there must be one polity on earth, so in heaven there must be one god who is worshipped under many names, in one religion which is a synthesis of all cults. These great concepts, vaguely formed though they are, and a supreme faith in his own destiny combine to make the Alexander of Pseudo-Callisthenes Romance a colossal figure.

II

A CHRISTIAN GREEK ROMANCE: THE ACTS OF PAUL AND THECLA

IN THE first three centuries of the Roman Empire one of the most popular forms of literature was the Greek romance.[1] These novels, written in Greek, fall into different types according to their prevailing color : love romances, the pastoral love romance, the historical romance, novels of adventure, the satiric romance. To these pagan romances must be added two Christian stories, written like the pagan in Greek and dating from the same period. These are the *Acts of Paul and Thecla* and the *Acts of Xanthippe and Polyxena.* These apocryphal writings about the saints deserve consideration because they reflect the popular interests of the early Christians and represent the stories they were reading in the first three centuries of our era. Also they have so many points in common with the pagan Greek romances of the times that they were probably influenced by them.

In a recent work Martin Braun has illuminated the significance of the rise of the Greek popular romance in Hellenistic times. The tension between Greeks and Orientals under the Greek rule made the Oriental long "for edification and consolation, for the revival of his self-

[1] Elizabeth H. Haight, *Essays on the Greek Romances,* New York, 1943. I am indebted to Prof. Grace H. Macurdy for suggesting to me this study of the Christian novels; and to Prof. Agnes Ringe and Prof. Adolf Katzenellenbogen for invaluable aid about the use of the story of Thecla in art.

esteem and pride, for appeasement of his hatred and contempt, or, where the tensions were less acute, for equality with the ruling people."

"History becomes legend and myth. Legends grow and are combined together to form something which can be called romance. This popular narrative literature is the spiritual bread without which no proud people can stand the pressure of alien domination, and it is individual heroic figures in whom the feeling and longing of the masses comes to a concentrated expression." [2]

What Braun says about the rise of the Oriental-Greek romance in Hellenistic times applies equally to the Greek romance in the early Roman Empire. And his analysis of the contents of such works as the *Testaments of the Twelve Patriarchs* describes the emotional coloring of the two Christian novels of the early Empire which we are about to consider:

"Morality centering around questions of sex-life is an ever-recurring theme"; we see "the painful conflict of the human spirit in late antiquity, when men and women, terrorized by the demon of sensuality, took refuge in penitence, asceticism and monastic life." [3]

The earlier of the two Christian novels I am presenting is the *Acts of Paul and Thecla*. The translators and editors of the Ante-Nicene fathers say of it :

"This book is of undoubted antiquity. There seems reason to accept the account of it given by Tertullian that it was written by an Asiatic presbyter in glorification of St. Paul (who, however, unquestionably occupies only a secondary place in it), and in support of the heretical opinion that women may teach and baptize. It is expressly mentioned and quoted by a long line of Latin and Greek Fathers." . . . "The text was first edited in 1698 by Grabe from a Bodleian ms., republished by Jones in 1726. A blank

[2] Martin Braun, *History and Romance in Graeco-Oriental Literature,* Oxford, 1938, pp. 2-3.

[3] M. Braun, *ibid.,* p. 45.

in the Bodleian ms. was supplied in 1715 by Thomas Hearne from another Oxford ms. Tischendorf's text is from a recension of three Paris mss., each of the eleventh century." [4]

A brief summary of the narrative must precede discussion of it.

The *Acts of Paul and Thecla*

Now Paul, having fled from Antioch, was on his way to Iconium. He was accompanied by Demas and Ermogenes, who pretended to be his friends, but were really jealous foes. A man of Iconium, Onesiphorus, went out with his wife and two sons to meet Paul and kept watching for a man who would answer the description of him given by a friend Titus, "a man small in size, bald-headed, bandy-legged, well-built, with eyebrows meeting, rather long-nosed, full of grace. For sometimes he seemed like a man, and sometimes he had the countenance of an angel." [5] When Onesiphorus identified Paul, he at once invited him to his house and entertained him. There Paul preached "the word of God about self-control and resurrection," beginning : "Blessed are the pure in heart, for they shall see God ; blessed are they that have kept the flesh chaste, for they shall become a temple of God." And in his preaching he enjoined chastity on men and women alike as the sure guarantee of salvation on the last day.

Near the house of Onesiphorus lived a girl named Thecla, daughter of Theocleia, who was betrothed to a man named Thamyris. And while Paul was preaching, three days and three nights Thecla sat at the window of

[4] *The Ante-Nicene Fathers*, translated and edited by Alexander Roberts and James Donaldson ; revised by A. Cleveland Coxe, New York, 1916, VIII, p. 355.

[5] The Greek edition used is that of C. Tischendorf, *Acta Apostolorum Apocrypha*, Leipsic, 1851 ; the translations are from *The Ante-Nicene Fathers, op. cit.*, vol. VIII.

her home listening to his discourse on chastity and devotion, not eating or sleeping, only longing to see the apostle whose words she heard. Her mother sent for her fiancé Thamyris and begged him to see if he could not break the spell which the stranger had cast on her daughter. But neither his kiss nor his appeal to her love and her modesty could shatter her new overpowering emotion. So there was great lamentation in the house.

Thamyris going out met on the street Paul's two false friends, Demas and Ermogenes, and asked them for information about this stranger who sought to break up homes, and he learned from them that Paul preached absolute chastity as the only way to resurrection. Instigated by the traitors, the next morning Thamyris went to the house of Onesiphorus with officials and a great crowd and demanded that Paul be brought before the governor Castelius on the charge of having corrupted his betrothed so that she would not marry him. In the courtroom Thamyris denounced Paul to the proconsul on this charge. While Demas and Ermogenes were urging Thamyris to accuse Paul also of being a Christian, the proconsul prevented this by giving Paul a chance to defend himself. Again Paul proclaimed his faith in the living God, in his Son, and in the saving grace of holiness, of fear of God, of love of truth. The proconsul then ordered that Paul be put in prison until he had leisure to hear him more attentively.

At night Thecla bribed the door-keeper of her house to let her out by giving him her bracelets. She went to the prison and bribed the jailer by the gift of a silver mirror to let her enter. There all night she sat at Paul's feet and listened to his words with growing faith. There in the morning Thamyris after a frenzied search found her, rapt in ecstasy. All this was revealed to the gov-

ernor, who summoned both Paul and Thecla to the court.
There though he heard Paul gladly, he was influenced by
the mob who cried : "Away with the magician !" and had
him scourged and driven out of the city.   When Thecla
did not answer his request that she return to Thamyris
and when her own mother urged that she be burned in
the theater as an example to all women who were abjur-
ing marriage rites, the governor condemned Thecla to be
burned.

In the theater Thecla, as a lost lamb in the desert looks
for the shepherd, kept looking for Paul.   And she saw
the Lord sitting there in the image of Paul and believed
he had come to help her.   The pyre was built high for
her execution.   Making the sign of the cross she mounted
it and a huge fire was lighted, but God sent a great storm
so that the rain and hail extinguished the flames and
Thecla was saved.

Meanwhile Paul with Onesiphorus and his family had
taken refuge in a new tomb on the road to Daphne.   And
the children becoming hungry were given his cloak by
Paul and told to buy bread.   One boy, as he was buying
it, met Thecla, who told him she was seeking Paul.   The
child led her to the tomb, where she found Paul on his
knees, praying that the fire should not touch her.   Together then they rejoiced in the miracles of Christ.

Thecla then told Paul that she would cut her hair and
follow him wherever he went.   But he replied : "It is a
shameless age, and thou art beautiful.   I am afraid lest
another temptation come upon thee worse than the first,
and that thou withstand it not, but be cowardly."   Thecla
begged him to give her the seal of baptism that temptation
might not touch her, but Paul postponed the rite.

Then he sent Onesiphorus and his family back to
Iconium and took Thecla with him to Antioch.   As they

neared it, a certain Syriarch, Alexander, on seeing Thecla, desired her and tried to persuade Paul by gifts and presents to hand her over. But Paul answered : "I know not the woman whom thou speakest of, nor is she mine." Then Alexander seized the girl and embraced her on the street. But she met violence with violence, and crying that she was the handmaiden of God and a lady of high rank in Iconium she laid hold on Alexander, tore his robe, pulled off his garland and made him a laughing-stock. Because of her attack on the Syriarch she was condemned by the governor to be thrown to the wild beasts. She plead only that she might remain chaste until she died. A noble woman, Tryphaena, whose daughter was dead, took her home with her to protect her.

At the first exhibition of the wild beasts, Thecla was bound to a lioness, but the creature only licked her feet. Tryphaena took Thecla to her home again and begged her to pray that her dead daughter might have everlasting life. At the final exhibition of wild beasts, Tryphaena again accompanied her charge and Thecla offered prayers for her protectress and herself. The charge against Thecla was sacrilege, but the women kept shouting that it was the sentence which was impious. In spite of that she was stripped except for a girdle and lions, bears, and a lioness were loosed against her in the arena. The lioness defended Thecla against the other wild beasts until it itself was killed. Thecla stood praying among all the others. Then seeing a trench of water she threw herself in it to baptize herself on her last day. All thought that the seals in it would devour her, but they were struck dead by lightning. No beasts had power against her, not even the wild bulls when she was bound to them, and fire was used to infuriate them. The fire freed Thecla by burning her bonds.

But Queen Tryphaena had fainted at the awful danger to Thecla, and Alexander the giver of the games asked the governor to free Thecla, for Queen Tryphaena was a relative of Caesar, who would surely destroy their city if anything happened to his kinswoman. The governor then questioned Thecla as to why the wild beasts had not touched her and again she proclaimed her faith in the Son of God who was her Savior. The governor then gave Thecla her garments and said to the people : "I release to you the God-fearing Thecla, the servant of God." Tryphaena took the holy maiden home and gave her all her possessions. Eight days Thecla remained with the Queen and taught her household until almost all believed in the true God.

Thecla then went searching for Paul and dressed as a man she travelled until she found him preaching at Myra. There she told him that she had received the baptism and she shared with him Tryphaena's wealth for aid of the poor. Then she went to Iconium and she blessed the house of Onesiphorus where Paul had taught her. Thamyris was dead, but she told her mother that God had given her back her child and she bestowed on her mother Tryphaena's wealth. Having thus testified, she went to Seleucia and lived in a cave seventy-two years on herbs and water, teaching to many the word of God.

Certain men who were "Greeks by religion, and physicians by profession" sent wicked young men to corrupt her. For they believed her power over the wild beasts came from her virginity and the help of Artemis. But God saved her by opening the rock so that she escaped underground from their assault. Then she went to Rome to see Paul, but found he had departed from this life. Soon she followed him and was buried near the tomb of her master Paul. So ended her life of ninety years.

Such is the story of the *Acts of Paul and Thecla*. Before considering its characteristics as a Christian romance and its relation to its pagan contemporaries, we must review the evidence for its dating. The distinguished scholar, Sir William Ramsay, has analyzed the different elements in it and advanced a plausible theory of the construction of the original story and its different revisions.[6] Ramsay does not discuss the doctrinal aspect of the *Acta*, but simply states that there is the greatest difference among authorities in regard to it. He is concerned with the geography and the inconsistencies of the story. His position may be briefly summarized as this. The *Acta* goes back to a document of the First Century. The original document mentioned facts of history and antiquities which had probably passed out of knowledge before the end of the First Century and have only recently been rediscovered. It was altered by the growth of the Thecla legend.

The scene of the original tale lay in Iconium and Pisidian Antioch and the action belonged to Paul's first visit to Iconium. In the versions extant, Antioch of Syria has been substituted for Antioch of Pisidia through a misunderstanding of the topography. The extant *Acta* is probably the work not of one but of three authors.

Queen Tryphaena is so essential to the plot that she must have been in the original story. She is an historical character known from coins and inscriptions. She was daughter of Polemon, King of part of Lycaonia and of

[6] W. M. Ramsay, *The Church in the Roman Empire before A.D.* 170. G. P. Putnam's Sons, New York, 1893, Chap. XVI.

Cilicia, also of Pontus. She married King Cotys of
Thrace and had three sons who were Kings of Thrace,
Pontus, and Armenia.   She was cousin once removed of
the Emperor Claudius.   The facts of the *Acta* suit the
date A.D. 50 when Tryphaena was living in retirement,
her son Polemon had been made King of Pontus and
Claudius was reigning.   Ramsay believes that Thecla
"was a real person, and that she was brought into relations
with the greatest figures of the Galatic province about
A.D. 50 — viz. Paul, Queen Tryphaena, and the Roman
governor." [7]

Indications of revisions of the original story are clear.
One is the confusion of geography.   A second narrator,
probably the Asian presbyter mentioned by Tertullian,
confused Syrian Antioch with Pisidian Antioch and laid
the scene in Syria.   Moreover the two trials and attempted executions of Thecla before two Roman gov-
ernors mark the tale as unhistorical.   There was no Roman governor at Iconium.   The presence of one at
Antioch is explained by the holding of the *venatio* there.
Also there is no adequate cause for the trial at Iconium.
Thecla's refusal to marry was a social act and should have
been dealt with by her family.   The charge at Antioch
was sacrilege, for attacking a state official in his religious
robes as *agonothetes* of the festival.   Ramsay gives a
plausible reconstruction of the *Acta* of the First Century
and of a revision made about A.D. 130, probably by the
Asian presbyter who was said by Tertullian to have constructed the document by additions to older material.   He
thinks further changes were made before 300 to give
Iconium more prominence.

This Christian novel in its present form dating from

7 W. M. Ramsay, *ibid.*, p. 388. On Tryphaena see also G. H. Macurdy,
Vassal-Queens, Baltimore, 1937, pp. 41–48 and Plate IV, 8.

the Second to the Third Century at once invites comparison with the pagan romances which were being written in that period. Both pagan and Christian stories appealed to the same general interests of the reading public, love, religion, and adventure.   Thecla's love is transferred from her fiancé to Saint Paul when she hears the apostle preach and then is sublimated to love of the unknown God whom Paul declares unto her.   Just as the pagan heroines through every temptation preserved their chastity inviolate for their lovers, so the holy Thecla by resolution and by miracle consecrates her virginity to her Lord as the surest means of salvation and eternal life. Just as the cult of Apollo, or of Pan and the Nymphs, or of Isis dominated the Greek Romances so the worship of the Redeemer is the fundamental theme of the *Acta*.   Adventures are limited in range, but exciting in portrayal : travel in quest of the saint, persecutions, trials, ordeals, miracles.

The new position of women in the early Empire is as marked as in the Greek Romances.   Queen Tryphaena plays the same rôle as protector and patroness of the heroine that Statira does in Chariton.   Thecla travels, teaches, makes converts, indeed is a leader of people much as Chariclea is in Heliodorus.   In general the types of character in the *Acta* resemble those in the Greek Romances. Paul, Tryphaena and a Roman governor carry out the tradition of using historical characters which the Ninus or perhaps the Alexander Romance started.   Saint Paul is hardly a romantic hero in aspect or magnetism, but he gains a peculiar aura from his identification with God, who sometimes appears as a beautiful youth leading the saint, and sometimes is embodied in Paul's likeness.   This sublimation explains both Paul's fear of temptation for Thecla (or himself !), his ungallant denial of having known the woman and his unwillingness at first to let her share his wanderings. She is gradually detached from the human preacher to direct communion with God.

Paul has a true friend, Onesiphorus as in Xenophon Habrocomes has Hippothoos ; and he has also false friends, Demas and Ermogenes, as in Achilles Tatius Clitophon has Clinias. These are types common to all the novels of the time. The heroine Thecla is on the other hand completely individualized. The episodes in her story are similar to those of the Greek Romances of the time. She falls in love with Saint Paul at first sight on hearing him preach. So in Xenophon of Ephesus Anthia and Habrocomes at the festival of Artemis seeing each other for the first time in her temple were vanquished. In Heliodorus too Chariclea and Theagenes fall in love on meeting at Delphi at a religious ceremony at the tomb of Neoptolemus. Thecla visits Paul in prison as Anthia does Habrocomes and in Achilles Tatius Melitta does Clitophon. Reunion in a cave is a feature of both the *Acta* of Thecla and of Heliodorus. The miracle of salvation from burning seems taken for Thecla from Chariclea's miraculous rescue in Heliodorus. Ordeals and tests of chastity are common to the *Acta* and to Achilles Tatius. Common too to pagan and Christian novels are the devices of developing character by soliloquies and prayers, by speeches and sermons, by initiation into religious cults and the seal of baptism. All this goes to prove that in the Second and Third Centuries the Greek story-teller, whether pagan or Christian, used the same themes, episodes, and artifices, calculated to interest the reading public of the period.

Against this conventional background Thecla is portrayed in the most vivid colors. She was only seventeen when Paul came to Iconium to preach and she sat three days and three nights in her window listening to his words. Seventeen too when she bribed door-keeper and jailer with her jewels and visited Paul at night in prison, sweeping away all conventions to learn more of salvation. At seventeen she was able to resist the entreaties of her mother and her fiancé and devote herself to the religious life even though condemned to death in the flames.

She was eighteen when she joined Paul in his travels and was insulted on the street by the Syriarch Alexander. All her pride of birth came out when she told Alexander that she belonged to one of the chief families in Iconium and wildly attacked him to protect her virginity. Condemned then to be cast to wild beasts, she found a protector of her chastity in a great queen, who gave her the sympathetic understanding which her own mother had not offered. Saved again from destruction, she went out to preach with Paul's blessing, visited Iconium to become reconciled with her mother and to revisit the house of Onesiphorus where she first heard Paul teaching. Her fiancé was dead. And now at peace with all the world she retired to a cave in Seleucia and there lived as a hermit seventy-two years healing all the sick who came to her, a holy Bernadette of the early Empire. Her ardor, her devotion, her aspiration make her a touching figure even before she became a martyr. She is not merely a virgin saint, but completely virginal in spirit. Her sense of dedicated chastity is outraged when she is stripped and forced to stand in the arena nude except for a belt as her pitiful prayer shows :

"My Lord and my God, the Father of our Lord Jesus the Messiah, Thou art the helper of the persecuted, and Thou art the companion of the poor ; behold Thy handmaiden, for lo, the shame of women is uncovered in me, and I stand in the midst of all this people. My Lord and my God, remember Thy handmaiden in this hour." [8]

Sir William Ramsay points out the great value of the *Acta* as "the only extant literary work which throws light on the character of popular Christianity in Asia Minor" during this early time. "Thecla became the type of the female Christian teacher, preacher, and baptizer, and her story was quoted as early as the Second Century as a justification of the right of women to teach and to baptize." [9] But the *Acta* gives us more than this : it furnishes an early Christian romance of an ardent young convert who by conversion was turned from earthly love to the adoration first of a Saint and then of the Lord himself.

It is noteworthy that the language of the Bible colors the diction of the *Acta* as the language of Homer enriched Chariton and Xenophon of Ephesus, or the language of Theocritus filled Longus' pastoral romance. Obversely it was natural that early Christian prayers offered their petitions in the name of Thecla. Typical *commendationes animae* are these :

"And in the same manner in which you saved the most blessed virgin and martyr Thecla from terrible tortures, save the soul of this thy servant and let her enjoy soon the blessings of heaven" ; "Assist us as you assisted the apostles when they were chained, Thecla in the glow of fire, Paul in persecutions and Peter in floods." [10]

The life of Thecla was quoted constantly as an example for consecrated women in the first four centuries.[11] St.

---

[8] Given only in the Syriac version ; translated by W. M. Ramsay, *op. cit.*, p. 413.

[9] W. M. Ramsay, *op. cit.*, p. 375.

[10] Wilhelm Neuss, *Die Kunst der alten Christen*, Augsburg, 1926, pp. 30–31.

[11] Sister M. Rosamond Nugent, "Portrait of the Consecrated Woman in Greek Christian Literature of the First Four Centuries" in *The Catholic University of America Patristic Studies*, vol. LXIV, Washington, 1941, pp. 36, 77–78, 81–82.

Gregory of Nazianzus in his *Exhortatio ad virgines* tells them to fear nothing :

> "A raven will nourish you just as it did Elias in the desert.
> You see Thecla escaping from the beasts,
> Paul eagerly suffering greatly and shivering with cold,
> That you may know, O Virgin, to look only to God."

Fourth-century encomia of her follow the tradition of her life in the *Acta*. As Sister M. Rosamond Nugent has pointed out :

> "She is lauded for refusing to marry a wealthy nobleman in order to labor with Paul in spreading the Gospel. God rewarded her contempt of the terrestrial even in this life, and in Heaven, crowned with glory, she stands near Christ . . . St. Methodius singled her out for special honors in the *Symposium*. It is she who leads the song of triumph and petition that concludes the dialogue. Her versicle is always the same :
> 'I keep myself pure for Thee, O Bridegroom, and holding a lighted torch, I go to meet Thee.'
> In the life of St. Syncletica "parallels are drawn with the blessed Thecla : both have Christ for their Spouse, Paul for their bridal leader, and the Church for their bridal chamber."

Such invocations, such laudations were reflected in early Christian art. In a chapel of El-Kargeh, a city of the dead in an oasis of the Libyan desert, there is a fifth-century (?) fresco representing Thecla sitting as an eager pupil beside her teacher, Paul.[12] Another fifth-century picture with the same theme was found on the ceiling of a funeral chapel in El Bagauat. Here Saint Paul sits preaching as his gesture shows. Beside him sits Thecla (both identified by inscriptions) in a long-sleeved robe and veil. She is ravished by the sermon and absorbed in writing down Paul's words.[13]

That too was the moment selected for portrayal of

[12] W. Neuss, *op. cit.*, p. 54.
[13] Oskar Wulff, *Die Altchristliche Kunst* in *Handbuch der Kunstwis-* senschaft, I, Berlin, 1913, pp. 98–99, with plate 79.

Thecla by the elder Holbein in his great picture the *Paulusbasilika* now in the Augsburg Museum.[14] The multiplicity of scenes from episodes in the life of Paul from the vision on the road to Damascus through imprisonment, baptism, travelling, to execution presents a confusion of figures, bewildering in crowding and arrangement. But in the central panel under the painful crowning of the Lord with thorns and above the awful decapitation of the saint there is a quiet scene which is the center of all the rest as well as the motivation. Within a chapel Paul is preaching to a little group of rapt listeners. Outside at the bottom of the steps on a wooden chair sits a young woman who surely must be Thecla. Her back is towards us. She is garbed richly as befits her station with a heavy white head-dress, a bright fur collar, a dark green velvet robe, and the stateliness of her costume is belied only by the shining little nape of the neck of the young devotee. Thecla sits alone. There is more space about her figure than about any other in the whole composition. To her our eyes recur again and again, finding in her intense absorption, in her repose, the meaning of the whole painting. Thecla through the teaching of Paul has found salvation, peace, and eternal life.[15] This picture of 1504 has caught the inspiration of the *Acta Pauli et Theclae.*

More certain and elaborate illustrations of the *Acts of Paul and Thecla* are furnished by the great altar-piece of the Cathedral of Tarragona, the Spanish city of which Thecla was the patron saint. The altar, made of one piece of white marble measuring four by two meters is an illustration of what Wethey calls "the predilection for the grandiose" which "reaches its ultimate expression in the

---

14 Curt Glaser, *Hans Holbein der älter*, Leipsic, 1908, plate XXVI, opposite p. 72.

15 See C. Glaser, *op. cit.*, pp. 72–81.

great retables of Spanish churches extending from floor
to roof vertically, and horizontally spanning the whole
breadth of the apse." "The plan is an enlargement of
the Netherlandish altar in which each scene is enacted in
a box-like division." [16] The altar-piece was constructed
in the early Fifteenth Century under the auspices of Archbishop Pedro de Garriga. The sculpture was designed
and executed by Pedro Juan de Vallfongona and Guil-
lermo de la Mota. It is an illustration of that florid
Gothic style in which architecture, sculpture, and painting united to create such a masterpiece.

The design is simple. Against a Gothic framework
two stories of rectangular panels are arranged. In the
first story, these panels portray six scenes in the life of
Thecla. They are separated by Gothic niches in which
stand statues of prophets, apostles, and saints. In the
second story, are placed three colossal alabaster statues,
in the center the Virgin and Child, at the right of the
spectator Saint Paul, at the left Saint Thecla. Between
the statues are eight panels in two rows with scenes from
the life of Christ.

In the first story, the first and last scenes appear to be
Church services with an Archbishop officiating. The
other four represent the miracles in Thecla's life : from
left to right, Thecla in the flames, Thecla among the lions,
Thecla in the river among the serpents, Thecla and the
bulls. In all these reliefs, Thecla has a large circular
aureole about her head.

In the first scene Thecla stands on the pyre making the
sign of the cross with extended arms which angels support. Her eyes are fixed on heaven. In the flames about
her body are seen heads of the damned, — dead, contorted

[16] Harold E. Wethey, *Gil de Siloe and his School*, Harvard University Press,
Cambridge, Mass. 1936, p. 10 ; see also Marcel Dieulafoy, *La Statuaire poly-
chrome en Espagne*, Paris, 1908, p. 63.

faces with grinning mouths.   In the second scene, which
is set in the arena, Thecla kneels, her hands folded in
prayer.   At her left, the friendly lioness who proved her
defender is guarding her so effectively that three large
lions grouped about her are gently succumbing to sleep.
Above the lattice-work of the arena are seen spectators.
Probably Queen Tryphaena and Alexander the giver of
the games are the central figures.   In the third scene
Thecla stands in a river to baptize herself.   Her consciousness of her nudity is betrayed by the gestures of
Venus pudica.   The dangerous serpents in the water
have all turned tail and are fleeing from her.   Two spectators stand under trees on either side amid river reeds.
Panel four is packed with figures.   An upper line of
background shows buildings and trees.   Below, a crowd
is depicted with women in the background and a lower
group of soldiers and executioners.   At the left stands a
dignified bearded figure with a high conical turban or
crown who looks down at Thecla, perhaps Alexander
the Syriarch, or the Governor.   Thecla in the lower left
corner is seated on the ground, praying with folded hands,
looking upward.   Her ankles are already bound with
rope.   An executioner is securing the ropes to the bulls.
Other servitors are goading on the two bellowing bulls
at the right, but they refuse to drag Thecla to death.

In all these scenes Thecla is nude to the lower part of
her body in accordance with the traditional narrative of
the story.   The sculptors have carved the slight figure of
the young girl with sympathetic tenderness, emphasizing
her small breasts, her slender arms, her thin body.   Not
only her nimbus proclaims her sainthood but every gesture and expression indicate her holiness.   This emphasis
on her original purity is enhanced by the use of a celestial
blue in the painting of the alabaster.   Gold and blue

are the chief colors employed with some rose-madder for contrast. And the dominating tones of the blue of the sky and the gold of the sun may well connote, as Dieulafoy suggests,[17] a virginal and celestial atmosphere for the seventeen-year-old girl. Chastity and devotion are the keynotes of Thecla's story in literature and in art.

[17] M. Dieulafoy, *op. cit.*, pp. 66–68. For a general summary of the appearance of Thecla in art, see the article by Henri Leclercq on Saint Paul in *Dictionnaire d'archéologie chrétienne et de liturgie,* publié par F. Cabrol et H. Leclercq, vol. XIII, part 2, Paris, 1938, pp. 2666–99.

III

THE ACTS OF XANTHIPPE AND POLYXENA

THE second Christian Greek novel of the early Empire is the *Acts of Xanthippe and Polyxena.*   In it as in the *Acts of Paul and Thecla* Paul is the hero.   Its heroines are not so famous as Thecla, but the story is more diversified and offers rich ground for comparison with the pagan Greek romances.

The Greek text is preserved in but one copy, a Paris manuscript of the Eleventh Century, and was edited for the first time by Montague Rhodes James in 1893.[1]   References to the story are rare and the earliest dates probably from the Tenth Century.   This history of the *Acta* is very different from that of Thecla's, to which from the time of Tertullian on many allusions were made in antiquity.

The sources of the *Acts of Xanthippe and Polyxena* are traced by James to at least six early romances : the *Acts of Paul and Thecla,* the (Gnostic or orthodox) *Acts of Paul,* the *Actus Petri Vercellenses* and the *Acts of Andrew, Philip, and Thomas.*   Moreover, familiarity with the pagan romances is indicated by striking similarities in the episodes of the story.   The dating of the book is determined by the use of the *Acts of Philip,* which was written

[1] *Texts and Studies,* vol. II, no. 3, *Apocrypha anecdota* edited by Montague Rhodes James, University Press, Cambridge, 1893.

in the first half of the Third Century. Therefore the *Acts of Xanthippe and Polyxena* was probably written about the middle of the Third Century.[2]

In type the story is a religious novel as is Thecla's. Conversion, baptism, and sanctification are the main features. In structure it falls into two definite parts which differ in treatment and language. Part I (chapters I to XXI) is the simple, homogeneous story of Xanthippe's conversion by Paul to the Christian faith. Part II (chapters XXII to XLII) contains the stories of Polyxena and Rebecca and is diversified by many more characters and episodes. In this way it has a stronger resemblance to the pagan novels. The significance of this romance is that it gives a vivid picture of what early Christians were reading for edification and amusement. A condensed narrative of the story will show its character and flavor.

The Acts of Xanthippe, Polyxena, and Rebecca
Part I. chapters I–XXI

When the blessed Paul, "the truly golden and beautiful nightingale," was preaching in Rome, the servant of a noble Spaniard named Probus, who had been sent there on business, heard him and was greatly moved by his teaching. On his return to Spain, he wasted away with longing for the word of the Lord. He told his solicitous master that only one physician, who was in Rome, could heal him.

Probus' wife, Xanthippe, questioned the servant about this physician and learned of Paul's teaching and of the rite of baptism. And as the servant told her of the Lord, the idols in the house fell down at the word. Probus in his sleep was disturbed by the Devil because the knowledge of God had entered his home.

---

[2] M. R. James, *op. cit.*, pp. 47–54.

Now Xanthippe like the servant began to waste away with longing for the word, with sleeplessness, with abstinence, and she prayed to the unknown God. Her husband Probus asked her why she could not sleep, saying : "And what is thy pain or grief, O lady, that I am not sufficient to comfort thee ? All that thou hast wished unto this day I have served thee in, and now what is it that thou hast, and dost not tell me ?".[3] Xanthippe begged that she might sleep alone one night and this he granted. All that night Xanthippe prayed to God if haply she might find him, and she said :

"Behold now, Lord, I cannot find any one that has love for thee, that communing with him I might even a little refresh my soul. Speed therefore, Lord, to yoke me in desire for thee, and keep me under the shadow of thy wings, for thou alone art God, glorified to all eternity."

In the morning Probus saw her eyes red from weeping and begged to help her, but she told him no man could ease her pain. So he went in great distress to receive the chief men of the city at his *salutatio*. And Xanthippe went into the garden and seeing the beauty of the world and hearing the songs of birds wished that she too might know the creator whom all nature was praising. And when Probus came home and found her still distraught, he fell upon his couch lamenting : "Alas, that I had not even the consolation of a child from her, but only acquire grief upon grief. Two years are not yet full since I was wedded to her, and already she meditates divorce."

Xanthippe was always looking through the door of the house unto the street waiting for the coming of some one. One day the blessed Paul arrived from Rome and Xanthippe saw him walking on the street. His kindly face,

[3] The speeches quoted are from the translation in *The Ante-Nicene Fathers*, Fifth Edition, vol. IX. New York, 1912.

his loving glance made her know he was a preacher and
she exclaimed that she longed to touch the hem of his garments. Probus on hearing her words rushed out to Paul
and begged him to enter his house to bring salvation
there. And they went in together to Xanthippe.

The eyes of Xanthippe's heart were opened so she read
upon the apostle's forehead in golden letters "Paul the
Preacher of God." At the revelation she threw herself
at his feet and burst into lyric welcome to the man of
God, her Savior. "Now," she cried, "I shall be called
happy by others, because I have touched thy hem, because
I have received thy prayers, because I have enjoyed thy
sweet and honeyed teaching." Paul told her that Christ
himself had sent him in pity of her to bear her mercy and
salvation. Xanthippe begged him to pray for Probus too,
to defeat the Devil's attacks upon him.

The fame of Paul's arrival brought many to the house
of Probus, who began to be annoyed at the crowds and to
say : "I will not suffer my house to be made an inn." But
the touch of Xanthippe's hand on his breast and her
prayer to God restrained Probus for a time. Presently
however the Devil won over Probus so he sent Paul away
and shut Xanthippe up in her bedroom. Another noble
of the city, Philotheus, at once offered Paul the hospitality
of his home. And Xanthippe heard where he had gone.

When Probus called Xanthippe to supper and she
would not come, Probus threatened her saying : "Think
not that in bed also thou wilt keep away from me." But
while he was at supper, Xanthippe prayed God to bring
sleep upon Probus until she should obtain the gift of holy
baptism. So Probus fell into deep sleep. Xanthippe
had the lights put out and then went to the porter with
three hundred pieces of gold to buy her escape, and when
the gold did not bribe him, she offered too her gem-

studded girdle and so gained her freedom. On flying feet she ran to the house of Philotheus, but at a certain place demons pursued her with flaming torches and lightning. Her prayers again saved her, for lo ! on a sudden Paul stood beside her and before him advanced a beautiful youth. And at that vision the demons fled. And Paul told Xanthippe that God had appeared in the form of man to give her courage against the demons. Xanthippe begged Paul to give her the seal of baptism, so that if death came upon her, she might depart to the God of compassion. So Paul led her to the house of Philotheus, there baptized her and gave her the bread of the eucharist for the remission of sins. Then Xanthippe returning home found that Probus still slept so she went to her bedroom and poured out her heart in ecstatic prayer. She begged Paul to come to speak for her. Yet something impelled her to go on : "My worthless mind delights me, and is not unfolded to the end."

Then while her eloquence continued, a cross appeared on the eastern wall and through it entered a beautiful youth surrounded by quivering rays and walking on light. The house shook. Xanthippe fell to the ground as if dead. But the youth changing to the likeness of Paul raised her and told her to fear not. And Xanthippe, believing him Paul, heard him speak gladly, but then from the radiance of his countenance she knew this was the Lord and she was sore afraid and fell upon the ground, acknowledging the divine presence. The vision vanished, but Xanthippe, coming to herself, was too weak to rise from the ground because of her fasting, the vision, and her lack of sleep.

Now in this night Probus had an alarming dream so in the morning going to the market-place he sent for two wise men, Barandus and Gnosteas, to interpret it. This

was his dream. In a strange country an Ethiopian king
was ruling all the world and driving all men to destruction. But suddenly above his head appeared a raven who
called pitifully. And from the east came an eagle and
seized his kingdom and all his followers fled to the eagle
who soared to heaven. Then a helper bearing a staff
came to the followers of the eagle and he washed them in
pure water and by his staff they conquered. And he sent
out men to all the world to bear witness to his work.
Barandus thus interpreted the dream. The Ethiopian
king is the Devil. The raven represents the weak people
of his kingdom crying for aid. The eagle summoned aid
from heaven in the person of the Lord Jesus Christ whose
staff is the cross. He baptized his followers and sent his
apostles forth to preach the word. Paul is one of these.
The dream is to admonish Probus to leave the king of darkness and receive baptism from Paul.

Probus was persuaded, but said : "Let us first go to
Xanthippe and see whether she still lives, for behold there
are twenty-nine days since she has tasted anything ; for
I saw her face in the evening, and it was as of one prepared to depart." They found her at home praising God
in song. And all went together to the house of Philotheus, where they found Paul teaching. Xanthippe fell
on her knees before Paul, then sat on the ground humbly
at his feet to listen. And Probus grieved at her humility
and, while Paul was teaching, had eyes only for her.

Paul was preaching this : "Let those that burn in the
flesh observe lawful marriage, avoiding fornication, especially that with another's wife, and let those that are united
keep to one another." Probus rejoicing asked Paul :
"Why then has Xanthippe withdrawn from me ?" Paul
said : "My son Probus, they that foresee that the works
of men shall be tried with fire, and that have always in

their mind the inexorableness of death, cast out all desire that cleaves to the flesh."

This was a hard word for Probus. He went home marvelling. That day he fasted. In the night he arose from his bed, saying : "Alas, how wretched was the day on which I was wedded to Xanthippe. Would that I had died and not seen her. I shall pray to the God of Paul. Perchance he will do to me also what is fitting, that I may not become a reproach in the world, being rejected by her." Then he prayed to God. Early in the morning he went to Paul, besought baptism and received it.

Xanthippe rejoiced and that night made a great feast in their home. But as she went up-stairs to her bedroom, a demon in the guise of an actor stood in a dark corner and tried to terrify her. She, thinking it was the actor whose jokes she had disliked and who had despised her as a woman, hurled an iron lamp-stand at his face and crushed all his features. The demon cried out : "O violence, from this destroyer even women have received power to strike us." Xanthippe was terrified.

Part II. chapters XXII–XLII

After supper Probus went to hear the word. Xanthippe stayed at home reading the prophets. Her sister Polyxena was lying on the couch. Xanthippe loved Polyxena because she was younger than she was and very beautiful. Probus loved her too. Polyxena had a terrible dream which she told her sister : a horrible dragon swallowed her beginning at her feet. But a fair youth appearing in the sunlight drew her out of the dragon, which disappeared. And the hand of her Savior was fragrant. Xanthippe interpreted the dream to mean that

Polyxena was dear to God and in the morning she must be baptized.

Then Xanthippe and Polyxena's nurse went to Paul. And while Polyxena was alone in her bedroom, a man of wealth and power, an enemy of her suitor, broke into the house and with the aid of demons, kidnapped Polyxena and took her off to sea. The bandits sailed for Babylonia, but the wind was adverse and the apostle Peter, passing them on a vessel en route to Rome, offered prayer for the soul in distress on the Spanish ship, for a voice from heaven had admonished him so to do.

The kidnappers after a violent storm landed in Greece and while all lay exhausted on the shore, the blessed Philip, sent by a vision, went down to the sea, found Polyxena and had her carried to the house of a friend to whom he intrusted the care of the girl. Her kidnapper, as soon as he recovered from his seasickness, went and demanded Polyxena, but her host would not give up his trust. So the bold robber raised an army and prepared to make war for the maid. Polyxena hearing this slipped away in the night. Her host was in despair, but his men raised an army and under the sign of the cross defeated the enemy.

Polyxena wandered away to lonely places in the hills where she sat down and lamented her cruel fate, kidnapped, left desolate, unbaptized. Finally, she found the den of a lioness which was empty and there spent the night. The lioness on returning in the morning respected her petition in the name of the God of Paul that the beast should not kill her until she had been baptized, and it kindly led her out of the wood to a highway.

There the apostle Andrew met her, and felt great commotion in his heart. But he prayed to God to calm his reason and was enabled to talk with the maid and help her to her heart's desire. For they found a well of pure water and there he prepared to baptize Polyxena. At the well they met a Jewish girl named Rebecca, who was a captive, sold for the third time. Andrew promised to baptize her also. Now as he prayed, the friendly lioness came running and, given voice by the Lord, abjured him to give baptism and instruction to the maidens. So Andrew rejoicing in the miraculous message from God baptized them both. They wished to follow him wherever he went, but this the Lord had not ordered, so Andrew told them to abide in peace, to remain together, to pray for him, and the Lord would save them.

Not knowing where else to seek refuge, they started for the haunt of the lioness. Then an ass-driver meeting them gave them friendly help and told them his sad story. He was a disciple of Philip and following the apostle's life he sold all he had and gave unto the poor. But his city rose against him and sought to seize him. God making him invisible, he escaped and now he travelled hoping to meet others of the faith. They asked him to take them to the sea so they might sail to Spain. And this he started to do. He gave wise advice to Polyxena : "Alter thy appearance to that of a man, lest for thy beauty's sake some one snatch thee away from me."

The next day on their journey a certain prefect seeing Polyxena had her carried off on his chariot though the ass-driver shouted : "A prefect does violence to none, why do ye this ?" But he was beaten and driven off. The ass-driver in great woe found Philip and told him all, and Philip cheered him by saying : "It is impossible for them to be dishonored, seeing that no one ever overcomes God."

The prefect took Polyxena to the city where he stayed and shut her up in a bedroom. A soldier seized Rebecca, but she escaped and found a kind old woman who hid her. Polyxena left alone offered prayer : "Woe is me, wretched one ; alas for me, miserable one ; now I know clearly how the Devil hates virginity, but O Lord Jesus Christ, God of all, since I dare not beseech thee of myself, I bring to thee the prayers of thy holy preacher Paul, that thou mayst not suffer my virginity to be destroyed by any one."

As she prayed, servants came to lead her to the prefect's bed. But Polyxena said : "Brethren, make not haste to any one's destruction, for this time shall quickly pass away, and they that work together with the destroyers shall perish with them. Rather assist strangers, that ye be not found strangers to the angels of God." The men ashamed told the prefect that the girl from fear had a high fever so he bade them leave her alone.

By night the son of the prefect came to Polyxena and again she was sore afraid. But he told her he was aware that she was the bride of God and this God he knew, "for," he said, "a certain man of glorious countenance lately in Antioch preached this God, and a certain maid, whose name was Thecla, believing him followed him, and encountered dangers on account of her beauty, of whom I have heard that she was condemned to the wild beasts." It was through the preaching of Paul that he had ceased to worship idols. The prefect's son planned to help Polyxena escape, but the prefect on learning of this condemned them both to be cast to the wild beasts. However, a lioness, loosed upon them in the arena, ran to Polyxena and licked her feet. In this miracle the prefect saw the hand of God so he saved Polyxena and his son. From them he heard the word of God and he and all the city believed. Polyxena now made preparations to go to Spain.

A certain man Onesimus who was sailing to Spain to Paul had a revelation, directing him to land in Greece, find two maids and a lad and take them to Paul. This he did after converting all the city of the prefect with the aid of a disciple of Paul named Lucius. After sailing twenty days, Polyxena was so exhausted they landed on an island for rest. Here fierce men, seeing Polyxena, attacked them to get the girl, but were driven off. Polyxena in terror had thrown herself into the sea, but the pilot saved her. In twelve days more they reached Spain. There Paul welcomed them. Polyxena besought Paul to deliver her from further troubles, but weeping he said : "Thus must we be troubled, my daughter, that we may know our defender, Jesus Christ."

Some one fetched Xanthippe and she seeing Polyxena fainted. When she recovered, she said : "I, my true sister Polyxena, went not forth at all for forty days, praying much for thee to the living God, that thy virginity might not be taken away. And Paul, the preacher of God, said to me, Her virginity will not be taken away and she will come quickly. And Probus said to me, It was assigned to her by God to be thus afflicted. Seest thou by how many devices God saves many ? But now, my beloved Sister, having unexpectedly seen thy face, now I shall willingly die."

Then Polyxena's kidnapper came and demanded her, but Paul converted him and also the suitor of Polyxena and there was great joy throughout the city on account of Polyxena's return. After that she never left Paul "in her fear of temptations."

In reading the story certain resemblances to the *Acts of Paul and Thecla* are at once noticed. There is only one direct reference to Thecla (C. XXXVIII) but there are similarities of details, episodes, and characters. These James has well summarized :

"Throughout the book . . . coincidences of thought are to be seen. In cc. VII, VIII Paul's first appearance is described : this should be compared with *Paul et Th.* 3. In c. XIII Xanthippe bribes her porter with gold and a girdle. Thecla c. XVIII bribes hers with her bracelet. The unsuccessful suitor Thamyris and Polyxena's more violent μνηστήρ are not dissimilar ; in both stories a ruler falls in love with the heroine and in both there is an unsuccessful exposure to wild beasts, and also a sagacious lioness ; the disparagement of the married state is a feature common to many of the spurious Acts." [4]

James goes on to show striking differences between Parts I and II of the *Acts of Xanthippe and Polyxena* in sources, character, and treatment. Part I uses four earlier *Acta* but the borrowed material is rather neatly covered. Part II uses two more *Acta,* quotes two directly and is "a much more obvious mosaic than Part I." In Part I the chief characters are three : Paul, Xanthippe and her husband Probus. In Part II added to these are Polyxena, Peter, Philip, Andrew, Rebecca, Polyxena's suitor, kidnappers, the ass-driver, a prefect, the prefect's son, Onesimus, who is the narrator of part of the story, and several minor characters. In treatment, Part I is much more concerned with the spiritual experience of Xanthippe than with external adventures. It contains nine speeches or prayers of some length. Part II is more like the pagan romances in being a narrative of exciting adventures.

Certain definite features of the pagan romances appear in both parts of the *Acta.* In Part I the beginning is religious, for the report which Probus' servant gives of Paul's preaching in Rome arouses Xanthippe's longing to know the living God through his servant. So Aphrodite's festival brought together Chaereas and Callirhoe in Chariton, the direction of the Nymphs associated Daphnis and Chloe on the hills in Longus, Artemis predestined Clitophon and Leucippe for each other in Achilles Tatius, and

[4] M. R. James, *op. cit.,* p. 48.

in Apuleius, Cupid, both god and lover, led Psyche out
of all tribulation to himself.   In all these stories divine
guidance seems to foreordain ultimate happiness.   Part
I shares too with the pagan novels the use of soliloquies
and prayers to deepen the subjectivity of emotional experience.   Xanthippe's new-found love of Paul and God
finds lyric expression in her prayers, her beatitudes, her
alleluias.   In describing her adoration of Paul, the servant of God, she portrays the symptoms of physical love :
the rapidity of the heart-beats, the desire to touch the beloved, even the hem of his garment, sensitivity to the sweet
odor emanating from his person.   The mysticism of her
ecstasies when fainting she falls to the ground in emotion
too great to sustain is paralleled by the mystic relations of
Lucius to the goddess Isis in Apuleius.

But Xanthippe not only experiences conversion and the
final dedication to the love of the new God ; she is not content until her husband Probus is pulled away from the
power of the Devil and the demons that beset him, and
like herself falls at the feet of Paul and receives the seal
of God's salvation, which is baptism.   Xanthippe has her
visions.   Probus has his terrifying dream.   And through
them as in the pagan romances finally safety is secured
and an happy ending out of all their misfortunes.   For
Xanthippe's story ends as brightly as any Greek romance
with Xanthippe and Probus united in love of Christ.
After Probus' baptism Xanthippe made a great feast for
all in the house to give them good cheer, because of her
great joy.   In general in Part I the resemblances to the
pagan novels are not so obvious as the happy ending.
Rather they are more subtle similarities arising on the
plane of intensified religious experience, manifested
through visions, dreams, conflicts between forces of good

and evil, and lyric expressions of communion, of beatitudes, of ecstasies.

In Part II the resemblances to the pagan romances are
more objective and more apparent. Just as in the Greek
love romances the plot centers on the long struggle of the
beautiful young heroine to preserve her chastity for her
lover, so in the *Acta* the dominant motif is the heroine's
aspiration to guard her chastity for God. In all attempts
to rape her, Polyxena sees an attack of the evil one and
exclaims : "I know clearly how the Devil hates virginity."
When Polyxena and Rebecca after their baptism are bidden by Andrew to remain together, living in holiness,
they forsake the haunts of men for the den of the lioness,
Rebecca declaring that it was better to live with wild
beasts than "to fall into the filth of marriage." On
Polyxena's safe return to Spain Xanthippe tells her that
she had prayed for forty days to the loving God that her
virginity might not be taken away. And though at the
end of the tale both Polyxena's suitor and her kidnapper
are converted and baptized, she chose the ascetic life and
"left not at all the blessed Paul in her fear of temptations."
Such was the result of Paul's exaltation of his own way
of life.

In episodes as well as in key-note the *Acta* resembles
the Greek love romances. There are repeated attempts
of rape on the heroine, but they are unsuccessful. Kid-
napping and dangerous sea voyages enliven the narrative.
Not only wicked men, but evil spirits, demons of the air,
assail the heroine's virtue. A multiplication of characters complicates the plot : assailants are doubled, help-
ful apostles are multiplied, various women give solace to
their kind. But there is only one devout lioness. This
wise beast, who finally through the mercy of God finds hu-

man voice, inevitably recalls Lucius the man-ass, his philosophical reflections, his final redemption. The rapid narrative ends happily in Polyxena's safe return to her home, her virtue unimpaired. Then unassailed by temptation she follows the blessed Paul in fear of temptations and finds the consummation of her life in sublimation of the love of man through love of God. The Christian Thecla, Xanthippe, and Polyxena attained their heart's desire as much as did the pagan heroines Callirhoe, Anthia, Leucippe, and Chariclea.

IV

A ROMANTIC BIOGRAPHY : THE
LIFE OF APOLLONIUS OF TYANA

PHILOSTRATUS' *Life of Apollonius of Tyana,* the Pythagorean philosopher and wonder-worker, is generally referred to by critics as a romance. This designation seems
to be adopted by them to distinguish the *Life* from reliable biography or true history. Phillimore declares
that the very title of the book and Philostratus' own statements about it prove that the author himself thought of
it as fiction. For the title τὰ εἰς Ἀπολλώνιον must mean in
English "In honour of Apollonius of Tyana" and Suidas
declared about the *Life* "It was *in his honour* that Philostratus wrote the Life of an Ideal Philosopher." [1] Philostratus himself in two significant passages refers to the
rhetorician's work in composing speeches for such a book.
As Phillimore points out "he makes Dio say to Vespasian,
'Restore the Republic, and afford us rhetoricians a topic
which will supersede Harmodius and Aristogeiton.' " [2]
And again when the trial of Apollonius under Domitian
is to be described, Philostratus admits that he must furnish the language of Apollonius' speeches and depict his
rôle in the court-room. [3] These are broad hints that

[1] *Philostratus in honour of Apollonius of Tyana,* translated by J. S.
Phillimore, Clarendon Press, Oxford,
1912, 2 vols., I. xv–xvii.

[2] V. 34, J. S. Phillimore, *op. cit.,* I.
lxxi.

[3] VII. 1.

81

Philostratus acknowledged he was composing fiction.

I propose now by an intensive study of the literary form and characteristics of the *Life of Apollonius of Tyana* to show that it uses the same technique as the Greek Romances of the early Empire, is indeed in purpose and structure a romance with a special orientation. As the title indicates, the interest centers not in a hero and heroine, but in one person. This hero is a Pythagorean philosopher. His quest is a philosophical way of life. His travels, whatever their *parerga,* are searches for new philosophical truths.

A review of the life of the author, his times, and the circumstances of his writing is a necessary introduction. We must ask who was Philostratus, how did the Empress Julia Domna come to give him a commission to write this book, who was Apollonius of Tyana, who was Damis, his *fidus Achates,* was he a real or fictitious character, did his memoirs actually exist ? After these considerations we will be ready to study Philostratus' *Life of Apollonius of Tyana* as a piece of literature.

Philostratus belonged to a family which included three or four generations of writers. Consequently there was confusion even in antiquity about the specific works which the individual Philostrati wrote. Probably our Philostratus was the Second, known as the Athenian, and he was the author of the *Lives of the Sophists,* some of the *Imagines* and the *Heroicus* as well as the *Life of Apollonius of Tyana.*[4] Both his birthplace and the date of his birth are unknown, though he may have been born at Lemnos in the reign of Commodus. By profession he was a sophist having studied rhetoric at Athens and Rome. In

---

[4] J. S. Phillimore, *op. cit.,* I. xxxiv–xlv ; Friedrich Solmsen, "Some Works of Philostratus the Elder," *T.P.A.P.A.,* LXXI (1940), 556–72.

the reign of Septimius Severus he was given a commission (he records) by the Empress Julia Domna to write the *Life of Apollonius of Tyana*. The work was apparently not finished before Julia's death in the east : after the introduction there is no further mention of her. Philostratus' own character and interests will be partly revealed through the structure and the style of the *Life* itself.

Julia Domna, the patroness of Philostratus, was one of the most spectacular of the Roman empresses. She was oriental in origin, daughter of Julius Bassianus, priest of the Sun at Emesa, Syria. The history of her youth is a blank, but after she married Septimius Severus in A.D. 187, her remarkable life vacillated between a struggle for political power and propaganda for philosophy. Her fame is attested by the fact that her coins exceed in number and variety those of any other empress, and inscriptions prove that she surpassed all her predecessors in the public honors she received.[5]

The facts of her life are significant. Astrology had a share in making her the wife of Septimius Severus if we may believe the tradition that her horoscope, which declared that she would be the wife of a king, lured Septimius to seek her hand. She travelled with her husband through the length of his Empire, from Asia to York, and everywhere was honored. But in Rome her very life was menaced when a jealous praetorian prefect, Plautianus, to check her political power, persuaded Severus to make her stand trial for adultery, which, for an empress, was treason. She was acquitted, but Plautianus had

---

[5] Henry Cohen, *Description historique des Monnaies frappées sous l'Empire romain communément appelées Médailles impériales*, Paris, 1884, IV, 104–39 ; Mary G. Williams, "Studies in the Lives of Roman Empresses. Julia Domna," *A.J.A.*, VI (1902), 259–305 ; J. McCabe, *The Empresses of Rome*, New York, 1911, 194–209.

to be appeased by the selection of his daughter, Plautilla, as the wife of Caracalla. The dominance of Plautianus was, however, shortlived and after his death and his daughter's, when Caracalla came to power, Julia regained her political prestige.

During the time of her persecution she devoted herself to learning philosophy and religion, became indeed the center of a literary circle of which Philostratus was a member. She had to endure new bitterness as a result of the rivalry between her sons, Caracalla and Geta, when by Caracalla's orders, Geta was murdered in his mother's arms. But accepting this new blow of fate she became the most influential political adviser of Caracalla and living with him in Asia acted as his chief minister both at Nicomedia and Antioch. After Caracalla's murder at Carrhae, Macrinus' succession, and his order to Julia to leave Antioch, she knew that the end of her power had come and killed herself. Later she was deified by Alexander Severus and inscriptions show that divine honors were accorded "to Julia Domna Augusta Pia Felix, Mother of the Emperor Antoninus Pius Felix Augustus and of the Camp and of the Senate and of her Country."

It was this highly colored, powerful Syrian empress who, Philostratus says, gave him the commission to write over Damis' memoirs of Apollonius of Tyana.

"There was a man, Damis, by no means stupid, who formerly dwelt in the ancient city of Nineveh. He resorted to Apollonius in order to study wisdom, and having shared, by his own account, his wanderings abroad, wrote an account of them. And he records his opinions and discourses and all his prophecies. And a certain kinsman of Damis drew the attention of the empress Julia to the documents containing these memoirs hitherto unknown. Now I belonged to the circle of the empress, for she was a devoted admirer of all rhetorical exercise ; and she commanded me to recast and edit these essays, at the same time paying more attention to the style and diction of them ; for the man of Nineveh had told his story clearly enough, yet somewhat awkwardly." [6]

In view of this circumstantial statement it seems curious at first sight that there should have been a long controversy as to whether Damis ever really existed. Yet common sense is bound to inquire where these memoirs had been for a hundred years and Damis' alleged accounts of Apollonius' travels, opinions, sayings, and discourses are so completely overlaid with the style of Philostratus, the sophist, that it is difficult to distinguish an embryo of genuine Damis tradition. Many scholars today agree with Eduard Meyer's contention that Damis is merely a fictitious narrator invented by Philostratus as a source, and so only a fundamental part of the structure of his romance.[7] I myself, while I am inclined to agree with Meyer, believe that the controversy about Damis is unimportant for our study of the *Life* as a piece of literature. The hypothesis that Damis is an invention of Philostratus does, however, strengthen the case for considering the whole *Life* a romance. As we study it, we shall see how carefully the character of Damis is delineated and how far removed from that character is the rhetorical presentation of the Pythagorean philosopher by the sophist Philostratus.

The life of Apollonius falls naturally in Philostratus' account into three periods of preparation, mission, and suffering. These are treated in very different proportions, for his early life with his birth and education is described in a few preliminary chapters.[8] His birthplace

---

[6] Philostratus, *The Life of Apollonius of Tyana*, I. 3. The translations of quotations from the *Life* are by F. C. Conybeare in *The Loeb Classical Library*, New York, 1912, 2 vols.

[7] For different view-points see J. S. Phillimore, *op. cit.*, I. xxi–xxii, cxvi–xxvi ; E. Meyer, "Apollonios von Tyana und die Biographie des Philostratos," *Hermes*, LII (1917), 371–424. [8] I. 4–19.

was the Greek city of Tyana in Cappadocia.   His father Apollonius was of an old and wealthy family.   Some would make him the son of Zeus because of the omens that attended his birth, for he first saw the light in a flowery meadow with swans singing and a thunderbolt soaring to heaven.

When the boy began to talk, he spoke pure Attic Greek and his beauty too was Greeklike.   His father gave him a good education first with Euthydemus, a rhetor, at Tarsus, then with Euxenus, the Pythagorean philosopher, at Aegae.   But young Apollonius helped direct his own education, for, the life at Tarsus seeming too riotous for him, he induced his father to let him move to quieter Aegae. And when at sixteen he found his teacher Euxenus no real philosopher, but a mere parrot repeating easily memorized phrases, he persuaded his father to install his teacher in a comfortable villa and let his son live in the temple of Aesculapius the true life of Pythagoras.

Here he devoted himself to the study of philosophy and to the establishment of a philosophical way of life.   He ate only vegetables and dried fruit and drank no wine in order to keep his mind and soul clear.   He wore only linen, went bare-footed, let his hair grow long, took only cold baths.   His prayer was : "O ye gods, grant unto me that which I deserve."   He began to teach even here in the temple, urging temperance in life and moderation in sacrifices so the gods approved of him.   At twenty when his father died, he divided the property with his elder brother and attempted to reform that gay young blade by his kindness and generosity.   He gave his own share of the family property to other relatives, keeping for himself a mere pittance.   And in this period of his life he took once for all a vow of chastity believing that only thus could he become a true Pythagorean.

To achieve that ideal he also imposed on himself a five years' period of silence, observing life, but never speaking, teaching his heart and tongue endurance. These years he spent in Pamphylia and Cilicia and after they were over, he went to Antioch in Syria where he lived in the temples, reforming their rites and teaching. Philostratus pictures for us a typical day in his life. He began the day with communion with the gods. Later he talked about the gods and the rest of the day he discussed the lives of men with his friends. At noon he would give some public discourse. Then he would refresh his body by an oil rub and a cold plunge.

The style of his speech was as simple as his life, without florid decoration, subtleties, or irony. His way of speaking was oracular, his sentences short and trenchant, his words fitting, his diction ringing. His object in life was to teach others the truths he had found.

With this sacred mission in mind and in quest of further knowledge he started upon extensive travels. Wishing particularly to visit the Brahmans in India, when his disciples tried to dissuade him from his daring adventure, in sadness over their softness and lack of courage, he bade them farewell and started forth with only two companions, a shorthand writer and a calligraphist. It was at Nineveh that Damis became his devoted pupil and after that with a zest for travel and a desire for wisdom accompanied him everywhere. "Let us depart, Apollonius," said Damis, "you following god, and I you." When Damis added that he could be of use because he knew many oriental languages, Apollonius declared that he himself knew all languages though he had never studied them. Nothing daunted, Damis went along and kept a scrupulous journal !

A chronological chart of Apollonius' travels would be

difficult to draw.[9] He spent a year and eight months in Babylon, visiting the Magi and expounding to the King his Pythagorean faith. Then he travelled over the Caucasus to India, was entertained by King Phraotes at his palace in Taxila for three days and finally attained the height of his desire in spending four months at the castle of the Brahmans, sharing their wisdom, observing their miraculous powers and demonstrating his own beliefs and miracles. Enriched by their wisdom, he returned to Babylon and Nineveh and at Seleucia took a ship for Ionia.

Now he lectured in Ephesus and Smyrna, stayed a plague at Ephesus, went to Troy and talked with the ghost of Achilles at his mound. His travels in Greece took him to Athens, Thessaly, Corinth, Olympia, Lacedaemon. He went to Rome and lived in the temples there until Nero expelled all philosophers from the city. Then he went on to Spain, returned to Greece for the winter, and in the spring set out for Egypt.

There his encounters with emperors began, for at Alexandria Vespasian, who had not yet seized absolute power, consulted the famous philosopher and it was to Vespasian that Euphrates and Apollonius presented in rhetorical discourses the rival claims of republic and monarchy. Apollonius' travels continued through Egypt and to Ethiopia : he saw the Nile and its cataracts ; he argued with the Gymnosophists, the naked sages of Egypt, about the comparative merits of their philosophy and the Brahmans'. After these travels, Apollonius was summoned to Tarsus by Titus, who had just taken Jerusalem, and who wished to secure from the philosopher the sort of

---

[9] For various attempts see J. S. Phillimore, *op. cit.*, I. cv–cxxvi ; Flinders Petrie, *Personal Religion in Egypt before Christianity*, New York, 1909, pp. 138–45. Phillimore criticizes severely Petrie's statement : "in all this mass of allusions to contemporary history and details of journeys, there is not a single misplacement or confusion."

valuable advice which he had given his father, Vespasian. Further wanderings took Apollonius back to the coast of Egypt, to Phoenicia and Cilicia, to Ionia and Achaia, to Italy. There under Domitian began the persecutions which tested his faith and his endurance.

For the theme of this seventh book of the romance is that a philosopher is tested by his action under a tyranny. And the culmination of the *Life* is the courage with which Apollonius endured imprisonment under Domitian and stood for trial before that emperor. Here is a new Socrates come to judgment, or, some would say, a new Christ. But Apollonius was not executed. (A Greek romance must end happily.) After his clear refutation of Domitian's charges, even before he delivered his *Apologia,* which was recorded afterwards, he vanished miraculously from the court-room and was transported at once against all limitations of time and space to Dicaearchia whither he had already sent Damis.

Again the master and the disciple travelled together, to Sicily, to Greece, to Ionia. At Ephesus by miraculous television Apollonius saw the murder of Domitian committed. Nerva on the throne summoned Apollonius to come and be his adviser, but Apollonius replied only by a letter which Damis bore. Damis was not to be allowed to see Apollonius' end, which the sage knew was near. No man knoweth his sepulchre, but his immortality was manifested by his appearance after death to a young follower to whom he delivered his final sermon.

After this résumé of Philostratus' narrative we are ready to analyze the technique of his romance. The theme is not love, adventure, and religion as in the Greek love romances, but a philosophical way of life. The title of the story contains a single name unlike the appellations of *Chaereas and Callirhoe, Habrocomes and Anthia, The-*

agenes and Chariclea, Clitophon and Leucippe, Daphnis and Chloe. There is no heroine in the novel, only a self-sufficient hero who has eschewed all sex and venery. The significance of this aloneness is revealed in the very first chapter which describes the life of Pythagoras, for two lines quoted from Empedocles are the key-notes of his personality :

"For erst while, I already became both girl and boy,"

and

"Rejoice ye, for I am unto you an
immortal God, and no more mortal."

Pythagoras is the self-sufficient *homo* ; he is also the superman, the θεῖος ἀνήρ, only a little lower than god. Apollonius was like his master. His isolated figure arouses only the sublimated devotion of disciples, of male disciples, for no women followers are mentioned. Where in the Christian *Acta,* Paul's story is nearer the Greek love romances in having a Thecla or a Xanthippe or a Polyxena for his worshipping votary, Apollonius has only Damis, the faithful secretary from Nineveh.

The adventures of the Greek Romances are repeated in the travelogue of the wandering Pythagorean and he (or Damis) records with interest the marvels of the countries through which they pass. But the real object of these travels is new philosophical knowledge, and, though Apollonius resided usually in temples, he was under the protection of no one god, but of a divinity above all gods. This is why through his unending search for wisdom he becomes a θεῖος ἀνήρ, very near to god himself. The eager Damis never attains this state, but his timid soul finally acquires courage to face imprisonment and even possible death through his faith in his master. Apollonius' mystic Pythagoreanism is put to an ultimate test against a pseudo-

historical background. For the great theme of the romance is finally the proving of the philosopher under the
tyrant. Domitian's persecution reveals Apollonius as indeed a man divine.

The technique of the narrative employs all the usual devices of a Greek romance : a special narrator, letters and
inscriptions, dreams and miracles, fine descriptions, lively
anecdotes, rapid narrative, court-room scenes, and epiphanies. Actually instead of one narrator, the author,
there are two narrators in the *Life,* Philostratus himself and
Damis. Achilles Tatius had attempted this device of the
double narrator in *Clitophon and Leucippe,* but had
failed to maintain the plan through his novel. Philostratus is more successful, for his Damis is ever-present
and is given a very individual character.

Damis joined Apollonius at Nineveh as a disciple because he was eager to learn wisdom, he was fond of the
road and wished to become a Hellene.[10] He hoped to be
useful because of his knowledge of many languages.[11]
His devotion made him keep a journal of their travels, of
Apollonius' opinions, discourses, and prophecies. This
was an accurate record, but written without charm.[12]
Damis had a practical sense that made him worry about
their physical needs. He was the one who informed the
Indian King Phraotes about the poor condition of their
camels and secured from the King both new beasts and a
guide. At Olympia Damis worried too about inadequate
funds, until Apollonius secured a sum from a priest in the
temple of Zeus.[13] His nature was essentially timid.
Now he warned Apollonius of the probable desertion of
his followers. Now he begged Apollonius not to go to
Rome for trial under Domitian.[14] Yet he never deserted

[10] I. 3 ; III. 43.
[11] I. 19.
[12] I. 19.

[13] II. 40 ; VIII. 17.
[14] IV. 37 ; VII. 13.

his master, accompanied him to Rome, shared his prison days and left him only when Apollonius sent him to Dicaearchia to await him there.[15] Apollonius, understanding Damis' terrors, encouraged him and instructed him by discourses on despising a tyrant, on realizing his own freedom of soul, on meeting death bravely.[16] Damis finally was able to tell a fellow-disciple Demetrius that, since he had found his master was divine, he had come to fear nothing while under his protection.[17] Apollonius' last words to his devoted pupil were significant : "O Damis, even if you have to philosophise by yourself, keep your eyes upon me." [18] This simple, devoted, ardent, adventurous disciple made an excellent second narrator for Philostratus' romance.

A device which the Greek Romances used to give an aspect of historicity to their narratives was documentation by letters and inscriptions. Philostratus uses many such pseudo-original sources. He quotes directly ten letters or groups of letters beside paraphrasing others. Some of these documents are mere letters of courtesy like the letter of King Phraotes introducing Apollonius to the sage Iarchas,[19] Apollonius' farewell letter to Iarchas,[20] his letter to Demetrius the Cynic appointing him adviser to Titus.[21] Others are on ethical or philosophical themes and significant for their point of view. One upbraided the corn-dealers of Aspendus for withholding corn from the starving populace.[22] A series of letters offered aid to the philosopher Musonius in prison.[23] Three letters to Vespasian rebuked him for his harsh treatment of the Greeks.[24] A letter to Titus commended him for his

15 VII. 15–41.   20 III. 51.
16 VII. 22, 30–31.   21 VI. 33.
17 VIII. 13.   22 I. 15.
18 VIII. 28.   23 IV. 46.
19 II. 41.   24 V. 41.

moderation after the capture of Jerusalem.[25] The style of these letters is laconic and pungent.

The narrative is further embellished by inscriptions, some of them fantastic in nature. Alexander's progress in India was indicated by altars which he set up dedicated : "To Father Ammon and Heracles his brother, and to Athena Providence and to Zeus of Olympus and to the Cabeiri of Samothrace and to the Indian Sun and to the Delphian Apollo." [26] Less authentic in aspect was the inscription on the tusk of a live elephant near Taxila who had fought bravely against Alexander and so had been freed by Alexander and marked with a Greek inscription : "Alexander the son of Zeus dedicates Ajax to the Sun." This elephant had fought three hundred and fifty years before ! [27] Equally droll was the inscription on a gold chain around the neck of a panther caught in Pamphylia, for the inscription was in Armenian, a dedication of King Arsaces to Dionysus.[28] Dionysus as well as Alexander visited India, for at Delphi a disk of Indian silver was dedicated with the inscription : "Dionysus the son of Semele and of Zeus, from the men of India to the Apollo of Delphi." [29] These inscriptions are, of course, the pure work of the Sophist.[30]

Surprisingly few significant dreams are reported considering that Apollonius spent much time in various temples of Aesculapius. Only two are dreams which Apollonius himself had. Near Babylon he dreamed that he saw fishes cast up from the sea on land raising a human lament and begging a passing dolphin to aid their plight "just like human beings who are weeping in a foreign land." Apollonius perceived that the fishes represented the Greek Eretrians who had been captives there for five

25 VI. 29.
26 II. 43.
27 II. 12.

28 II. 2.
29 II. 9.
30 E. Meyer, *op. cit.*, pp. 376–78.

hundred years and that by the dream the gods gave him a mission to relieve their wretched fate.[31] Again at Sparta in a dream a venerable woman appeared to him and asked him to visit her before going to Italy, for she was the nurse of Zeus, "and she wore a wreath that held everything that is on the earth or in the sea." By these words he knew that he was destined to visit the island of Crete.[32]

Three other dreams mentioned were about Apollonius. Just before his birth his mother was bidden in a dream to walk to a meadow and gather flowers. When she went there and fell asleep among the flowers, swans encircled her in a dance, singing, and at their song she leaped up and bore her child.[33] The King of Babylon before Apollonius' visit dreamed that he had been transformed into Artaxerxes, son of Xerxes, and he was terrified at what change of fortune this might signify. But when Apollonius arrived, he recalled that Themistocles the Athenian had visited Artaxerxes to the great benefit of both, so he perceived that this new Greek guest Apollonius would be a second Themistocles to himself.[34] During the trial of Apollonius under Domitian, at Dicaearchia where his disciples were awaiting him, Telesinus had a dream : "he saw a fire spreading like a sea over the land, and it enveloped some men, and caught up others as they fled ; for it flowed along, he said, exactly like water, but you alone suffered not the fate of the rest, but swam clean through it as it divided to let you through." This was interpreted by Telesinus as a good omen from the gods, about the safety of Apollonius.[35] These dreams, few as they are, reflect the belief of the times in regard to the significance of dreams and enlarge the mystic aura about the head of Apollonius.

[31] I. 23–24.
[32] IV. 34.
[33] I. 5.

[34] I. 29.
[35] VIII. 12.

Miracles, another feature of the Greek Romances, loom far larger in the *Life* than do dreams.[36] Apollonius himself is a wonder-worker although both he and his followers resent his being called a wizard or a magician. Part of his quest in his visit to the Brahmans was to observe their magical powers as well as to share their wisdom. They fought off enemies who tried to storm their castle by hurling thunderbolts.[37] They were aware of their past lives in former incarnations [38] and they had foreknowledge of the future.[39] Each had a ring and a staff with virtue to enable him to do all things.[40] They could use the magical Pantarbe stone.[41] At their banquets automatic bronze tripods served the food, which earth unlabored furnished.[42] They effected cures, healing partly by massage, but also by magic.[43] They knew something of astrology, for Iarchas gave Apollonius seven rings, named for the seven stars, which he wore in turn on each day of the week,[44] and Iarchas had proved himself the reincarnation of the Indian hero Ganges by discovering the seven swords of adamant which Ganges had fixed in the earth to ward off enemies.[45] The Brahmans' supreme magical power was manifested in levitation, for in their ritual they raised themselves two cubits from the earth in order floating in the air to commune more easily with the Sun-God.[46] These powers, except the control of automatic tripods and the levitation for worship, Apollonius was able to rival and outdo.

The sage of Tyana understood all languages of men though he had never studied them, also the languages of

[36] Lynn Thorndike, *A History of Magic and Experimental Science during the first thirteen Centuries of our Era*, New York, 1923, I. 242–67.
[37] II. 33.
[38] III. 20–22.
[39] III. 12.

[40] III. 15, 17.
[41] III. 46–47.
[42] III. 27.
[43] III. 39–40.
[44] III. 41.
[45] III. 21.
[46] III. 15, 33.

animals and birds.[47] He could heal a boy bitten by a
mad dog by making the dog obey his will, lick the wound
and drink running water to cure himself as well as the
boy.[48] Apollonius had power not only over animals, but
over demons, hobgoblins, and even a satyr. In the moon-
light near the Caucasus he drove away a hobgoblin which
wished to interfere with their travels by cursing it
roundly.[49] He cured a boy of sixteen who was possessed
by a demon by addressing a letter full of threats to the
evil spirit.[50] He stayed a plague at Ephesus by having the
populace stone to death a demon disguised as an old
beggar.[51] He rid an Ethiopian village of the ghost of a
lecherous satyr by filling a fountain with wine and get-
ting him drunk.[52] And he saved a philosopher from a
vampire bride.[53]

Apollonius displayed foreknowledge of such different
events as the plague at Ephesus and the manner of the
death of the Emperor Titus.[54] By television he beheld
in Egypt the burning of the Temple of Jupiter Capitoli-
nus in Rome and in Ephesus witnessed the murder of
Domitian in Rome.[55] He showed power over inanimate
objects by withdrawing his leg from his fetters in prison.[56]
He overcame the limitations of space by transporting
himself in a day from Rome to Dicaearchia.[57] His ultimate victory was over death. Not only did he raise the
ghost of Achilles at his mound, but he himself ascended
into heaven and then appeared again to a young disciple
to reveal his glorious immortality.[58]

47 I. 19–20.
48 VI. 43.
49 II. 4.
50 III. 38.
51 IV. 10.
52 VI. 27.
53 IV. 25. For a rationalization of
the myths of certain of Apollonius'
miracles (the staying of the plague at
Ephesus, the exposure of the vampire
bride) see Legrand d'Aussy quoted in
A. Chassang, *Apollonius de Tyane*,
Paris, 1862, pp. 444, 447–50.
54 IV. 4 ; VI. 32.
55 V. 30 ; VIII. 25–26.
56 VII. 38.
57 VIII. 5, 10.
58 IV. 11, 15–16 ; VIII. 30, 31.

In spite of all these manifestations of miraculous powers, Apollonius defended himself in his *Apologia* against the charges of wizardry and divination.[59] He claimed that he could foretell the future because he was a Pythagorean and pure in heart.[60] Through wisdom a man may have something of god in him. Such a man, purifying his body by light diet, scorning all avarice, praying to the gods for help, may foresee the future and without sacrifices of the blood of animals or human beings may become a savior of mankind.[61]

This recurring theme of the θεῖος ἀνήρ will be met again in a study of Apollonius' discourses. Now we must proceed to a further consideration of the resemblances of Philostratus' technique to that of the other Greek Romances. In descriptions and anecdotes he rivals them. His descriptions often focus on marvels of natural science seen in Apollonius' travels, which were the delight of the times, like the elephants and the dragons of India.[62] "Julia's Court," says Phillimore, "loved Encyclopedias — so there must be plenty of tidbits of science, geography, physics, and zoology."[63] No more lively and sympathetic account of elephants' intelligence, tricks, care for their young, *esprit de corps,* service for man was ever written. A little elephant boy of thirteen too has his share in the vivid picture.

A more imaginative and stately description is that of the castle of the sages in India.[64] For this Acropolis is surrounded by clouds which make the sages visible or invisible at their pleasure. It has a mystic well discharging blue light shot with a rainbow and a crater of purifying fire, jars of the rains and the winds, self-kindled fire and eternal sunlight, and everflowing springs of living water.

[59] VIII. 7.
[60] VI. 11.
[61] VIII. 7.
[62] II. 11–16; III. 6–8.
[63] J. S. Phillimore, *op. cit.*, I. lxxii.
[64] III. 13–15.

Here in pictures of elephants and of castle are illustrations of two extremes of realistic and imaginative descriptions.

Philostratus' narrative art appears no less in the recounting of anecdotes. These vary from fables worthy of Aesop to a grisly tale of a vampire bride and the tragedy of a young Egyptian Hippolytus. Memorable is the little gem about the communistic sparrow who finding some spilled grain at once flew off to summon a flock of friends to the feast, a lesson in sharing for mankind.[65]

The most famous story of Apollonius, says Philostratus, is the tale of Menippus and his vampire bride.[66] It was at Corinth that young Menippus lived, looking like a beautiful young athlete, but really a student of philosophy. Once on the road to Cenchreae he met a fair Phoenician woman who took his hand, declared that she had loved him long and invited him to come to her home near Corinth. "When you reach the place this evening," she said, "you will hear my voice as I sing to you, and you shall have wine such as you never before drank, and there will be no rival to disturb you ; and we two beautiful beings will live together." Menippus, philosopher that he was, accepted her invitation and fell madly in love with the lady, never dreaming she was a mere apparition.

Apollonius, however, recognized the creature and tried to save Menippus by telling him his innamorata was a serpent. But Menippus went on with preparations for his marriage next day. Apollonius appeared at the wedding and found the house magnificently decorated with a great display of gold and silver. Menippus admitted that all the splendor was the lady's, for his wealth consisted only in his philosopher's cloak. Apollonius proceeded to blow the woman down, for when he declared that the bride was one of the amorous empusas, lamias, or hob-goblins who feed on young men, all the gold and silver, all the wine-bearers and the cooks vanished. Finally the bride before the stern rebukes of Apollonius wept and confessed that she was a vampire and that she was fat-tening up Menippus to devour him with more pleasure. That is the way in which Apollonius saved a young disci-ple from a lamia at Corinth. A good story this with its realistic descriptions, its conversations, its magic, and its moral ending. The same liveliness of narrative appears in the anecdote of the young girl whom Apollonius raised from the dead,[67] and the account of how a young Egyptian Hippolytus resisted his step-mother.[68] These gems of inset stories enrich the narrative just as they do in the Greek love romances.

Rhetorical speeches and court-room scenes are also part of the conventions of the Greek Romances, but in Philo-stratus they play a pivotal part in developing the character of his hero. When Vespasian in Egypt consulted Apol-lonius about his future rule in Rome, Euphrates made a long plea for the restoration of the Roman Republic, but Apollonius favored a beneficent monarchy, for "the gov-ernment of one man, if it provides all round for the wel-fare of the community, is popular government." [69] Here are themes as clearly part of the sophist's stock in trade as those of the traditional *suasoriae* : "Hannibal deliberates whether to attack Rome," "Ajax soliloquizes before his suicide," "Cicero refuses to recant his Philippics." As Phillimore says,

"Philostratus lets the cat out of the bag when, in one of the most undisguisedly academic passages of the book (that old 'set-piece,' the Respective Merits of Monarchy and Democracy), he makes Dio

[67] IV. 45.
[68] VI. 3.
[69] V. 28–36.

say to Vespasian, 'Restore the Republic, and afford us rhetoricians a topic which will supersede Harmodius and Aristogeiton.' " [70]

But the theme of these "set-pieces" is significant for Philostratus' whole *Life* of Apollonius. Here the sage supports monarchy because he believes it can be democratic. Near the end of his life when he came to trial under Domitian, he was put to a test which Philostratus declares is the true test of a philosopher, namely how he behaves under tyranny. And his trial in the court-room over which Domitian presided and his *Apologia* for his life attest the dignity and nobility of his proving. [71]

It was indeed a noble way of life that Philostratus put forth through Apollonius' teachings rather than a carefully elucidated system of philosophy. [72] And in the court-room scene before Domitian it is that way of life which is on trial. Four questions the Emperor put to him, four that the sage easily answered :

" 'What induces you, Apollonius, to dress yourself differently from everybody else, and to wear this peculiar and singular garb?' 'Because,' said Apollonius, 'the earth which feeds me also clothes me, and I do not like to bother the poor animals.' The Emperor next asked the question : 'Why is it that men call you a god ?' 'Because,' answered Apollonius, 'every man that is thought to be good is honoured by the title of god.' . . . 'What motived,' he said, 'or suggested your prediction to the Ephesians that they would suffer from a plague ?' 'I used,' he said, 'O my sovereign, a lighter diet than others, and so I was the first to be sensible of the danger.' "

When Domitian came to the fourth question, which was on Apollonius' relation to Nerva and his friends, he put it in such an indirect way that Apollonius was able to an-

[70] J. S. Phillimore, *op. cit.*, I. lxx–lxxi.

[71] VIII. 1–7.

[72] A. D. Nock, *Conversion*, Clarendon Press, Oxford, 1933, p. 129. "What Philostratus offers is a paganism interpreted by philosophy and approximating to a religious system. In this Life, and in the *Heroicus* . . . there is a clear rise in the tension of piety."

swer by demanding witnesses of the charges implied. The whole audience became witnesses by applauding so Apollonius was acquitted. Apollonius then boldly denounced Domitian's misrule, told him, if he wished, to seize his body for he never could take captive his soul, and then declared that the Emperor could not seize even his body, for in the words of Homer :

"Thou shalt not slay me, since I tell thee I am not mortal."

Then as if to prove his words, Apollonius vanished from the court-room. He never delivered the real defense which he had written. Philostratus published it afterwards.[73]

The *Apologia* is a carefully prepared rhetorical speech. It expands his rebuttal of attacks on his garb and his diet and reaffirms his horror at blood sacrifices. It contains no very convincing arguments against the charges of wizardry and of association with Domitian's enemies, a conspiracy with Nerva and his friends. Against wizardry, Apollonius uses the fact that Vespasian consulted him about his plans for ruling : he never would have done this had Apollonius been a wizard. Moreover, wizards work for personal gain, and Apollonius is above suspicion in regard to avarice. His power over demons and his foreknowledge came not from magic, but from the help of the gods.

As for his relations to Nerva, he boldly praises him as "a man worthy of the highest office and of all the consideration that belongs to a good name and fame," but he declares that "his frame is undermined by a disease which fills his soul with bitterness and incapacitates him" both for home duties and affairs of state : for so ill a man ambition for empire is impossible.

[73] VIII. 5–7.

The *Apologia* attempts to portray Apollonius' way of life, but to complete the picture of his teachings we need to survey all the discourses which Damis-Philostratus reported. Apollonius defined his wisdom once as "an inspiration which teaches men how to pray and sacrifice to the gods." [74] Damis reported the "great subjects" on which Apollonius talked : the matter of rites and ceremonies and their reform ; [75] "the most profitable topics, such as wisdom and courage and temperance, and in a word upon all the virtues." [76] Through many such discourses and through incidental conversations we can reconstruct his creed. He believed in the continuity of life attained through the transmigration of souls, the self-sufficiency of the philosopher and his chastity, his peculiar garb to set him off from other men, his light diet to keep his mind clear and his soul pure, a wealth that consisted in spiritual possessions, supernatural powers obtained through communion with god, and, finally, a share in divinity itself which made him a θεῖος ἀνήρ, a savior of mankind.

From this assured faith, he dared make his great appeal to Domitian at the end of his *Apologia* :

"The prosperity of men runs in a circle, and the span of happiness, my prince, lasts for a single day. My property belongs to another and his to another, and his again to a third ; and each in having hath not. Think of this, my prince, and put a stop to your decrees of exile, stay the shedding of blood, and have recourse to philosophy in your wishes and plans ; for true philosophy feels no pangs. And in doing so wipe away men's tears ; for at present echoes reach us from the sea of a thousand sighs, and they are redoubled from the continents, where each laments over his peculiar sorrows. There is bred an incalculable crop of evils, all of them due directly to the slanderous tongues of informers, who render all men objects of hatred to yourself, and yourself, O prince, to all." [77]

[74] IV. 40.   [76] IV. 31.
[75] IV. 19.   [77] VIII. 7.

Even after his death Apollonius returned to convince a sceptical young disciple that he still lived. In oracular hexameters he proclaimed :

> "The soul is immortal, and 'tis no
> possession of thine own, but of Providence,
>   And after the body is wasted away,
> like a swift horse freed from its traces,
>   It lightly leaps forward and
> mingles itself with the light air,
>   Loathing the spell of harsh and
> painful servitude which it has endured.
>   But for thee, what use is there in this ?
> Some day when thou art no more thou
> shalt believe it.
>   So why, as long as thou art among
> living beings, dost thou explore these mysteries ?" [78]

Philostratus ends his romance with a comment on these words :

> "Here we have a clear utterance of Apollonius, . . . to convince us of the mysteries of the soul, to the end that cheerfully, and with due knowledge of our own true nature, we may pursue our way to the goal appointed by the Fates." [78]

The style in which Apollonius expressed himself in his formal speeches and informal teaching has been well characterized by Philostratus :

> "The literary style which he cultivated was not dithyrambic or tumid and swollen with poetical words, nor again was it far-fetched and full of affected Atticisms. . . Neither did he indulge in subtleties, nor spin out his discourses ; nor did anyone ever hear him dissembling in an ironical way, nor addressing to his audience methodical arguments. . . His sentences were short and crisp, and his words were telling and closely fitted to the things he spoke of,

[78] VIII. 31. On Apollonius as "the philosophic theologian" and his teachings see S. Dill, *Roman Society from Nero to Marcus Aurelius*, London, 1911, pp. 346–47, 399–401, 518–20 ; for a satiric view of Philostratus' fiction see B. L. Gildersleeve, "Apollonius of Tyana," in *Essays and Studies*, Baltimore, 1890, pp. 251–96. Gildersleeve wrote as derisively of Apollonius as Lucian did of Alexander of Abonoteichus.

and his words had a ring about them as of the dooms delivered by a sceptred king." [79]

He affirmed that as a youth he had asked questions : now it was his business to teach people what he had discovered.[79] This is a fair account of Apollonius' style and aims.   But when Philostratus analyzes the style of the *Apologia,* he is not so good a critic, for he wishes to exalt the philosopher and conceal the rhetorician.

"Those who highly esteem the style of buffoons will find fault with it, as being less chaste and severe in its style than they consider it should be, and as too bombastic in language and tone. However, when I consider that Apollonius was a sage, it seems to me that he would have unworthily concealed his true character, if he had merely studied symmetry of endings, and antithesis, clicking his tongue as if it had been a castanet. . . When a wise man is defending his cause . . . he requires quite another style than that of the hacks of the law-court ; and though his oration must be well-prepared, it must not seem to be so, and it should possess a certain elevation almost amounting to scorn." [80]

It is difficult for modern readers to feel that in Apollonius' *Apologia* the philosophical elevation thus dominates over the rhetorical structure.   Actually, the style of Apollonius is the style not of the sage of Tyana but of the sophist of Lemnos as Eduard Meyer has pointed out. Meyer does not limit his strictures to the style of the *Apologia.*   He analyzes the whole of Philostratus' narrative, and points out that the entire first part, the trip into the Orient to the Indian sages, is imaginary and unhistorical.   It is the pure work of the sophist just as much as are the learned conversations which Apollonius carries on with Phraotes, Iarchas, Damis.   One proof is that subject matter and style are one.   Philostratus never could have rewritten Damis' narrative in this rhetorical

style.   Another proof that this is all the creation of Philostratus is the interest in Greek literature, music, and
works of art which is characteristic of the whole romance.
This is certainly due, not to the fictitious Damis, but to
Philostratus, the *rhetor* and the author of the εἰκόνες.[81]

Of the Greek authors used, Homer stands at the head.
Many episodes from the *Iliad* and the *Odyssey* are used
and the Homeric Achilles in person reappears as a shade
near his mound.[82]   There are many incidental references
to Homer and his lines are constantly quoted.[83]   Even in
the court-room Apollonius ends his speech with thoughts
on death from the *Oedipus Coloneus* and the *Odyssey*.[84]

The tragedians too are often in Apollonius' thoughts.
He delivers a long account of Aeschylus' pioneer work in
developing tragedy.   He quotes from Sophocles not only
the *Oedipus Coloneus,* but the *Oedipus Rex* and the *Antigone*.[85]   Lines from Euripides' *Andromache, Orestes,*
and *Bacchae* spring to his lips.[86]   He refers to Pindar's
praise of the lyre and to Archilochus' praise of patience.
While Pythagoras is the backbone of his philosophy, he
mentions Plato and many other Greek philosophers.   He
quotes Demosthenes' *On the Crown*,[87] and he instructs
Damis at length about Aesop's great gifts in teaching
ethics through stories of animals.[88]

References to music are not so numerous as those to
literature.   The moral effects of the music of the flute
and of the lyre are mentioned.[89]   Hymns to the king of
India and the chorus of the Brahmans to god, sung as they
poised suspended in a circle in the air, are described.[90]

[81] E. Meyer, *op. cit.*, pp. 372–79.
[82] IV. 11–16.
[83] III. 6, 19, 22, 27 ; IV. 38 ; VI. 31 ;
VII. 14, 22 ; VIII. 5, 7, 13.
[84] VIII. 7.
[85] VII. 4; IV. 38.
[86] II. 14; VII. 14; IV. 21.
[87] VII. 37.
[88] V. 14–15; VII. 30.
[89] IV. 21 ; VII. 12 ; V. 21.
[90] III. 33 ; III. 17.

And stinging satire is launched against Nero as a patron of musical contests and as a singer and a player of the zither.[91] Such travesties are desecration.

Interest in works of art is much more intense. The objects described include sculpture and painting, their subjects, their technique. Philostratus never loses an occasion to comment on the art of the countries through which Apollonius passes or to compare Oriental art with the Greek. Miraculous works of art too are described with a naïve delight in the marvels of fairy lore. Automatic tripods of black brass fashioned as cupbearers serve wine and water to the guests of the Brahmans.[92] A statue of Tantalus, metamorphosed into the friend of men, bears a magical cup of ever-flowing water, from which the Indian sages and their guests drink a draught of friendship.[93] In Ethiopia there is a seated statue in black stone of Memnon of the Dawn, and though the style is archaic, it was so made that when the sun at rising touched the face, the lips spoke and the eyes gleamed.[94] In Babylon there are golden tapestries and pictures made of solid gold, depicting Greek myths and Greek battles. And there a house has a dome of sapphire representing the sky and in it hang as though floating in ether shining golden images of the gods.[95] The statues of the Greek gods made in the image of man are exalted over the animal-headed Egyptian deities,[96] for had not Apollonius seen the Dionysus on Nysa, the Aphrodite at Paphos, the Zeus at Olympia?[97] Statues of heroes too are mentioned : Leonidas in Thessaly, Alexander near Taxila standing in an eight-horse chariot on top of a triumphal arch.[98] The subjects and technique of various Greek reliefs are also

[91] IV. 24, 39, 42 ; V. 7.
[92] III. 27.
[93] III. 25, 32.
[94] VI. 4.

[95] I. 25.
[96] VI. 19.
[97] II. 8 ; III. 58 ; IV. 28.
[98] IV. 23 ; II. 42.

described : in the Temple at Taxila bronze reliefs of the exploits of Alexander and Porus, all wrought in color through the inlay of various metals ; [99] in Spain an altar of stone to Heracles carved with his twelve labors.[100] And besides making a few incidental references to the technique of sculpture in the round and in relief, Apollonius holds a long discourse with Damis on the colors and technique of painting and at another time uses as an illustration of famous painting Prodicus' picture of the choice of Heracles.[101]

All this interest in the arts is in character for Philostratus and not in character for the Apollonius who reveals himself through his extant Epistles.[102] The writer of these ninety-seven letters indeed is a different Apollonius from the one created by Philostratus. He is more violent in his hatred of Euphrates, a more severe critic of cities and of men. Only in his communications with his family does he show a more friendly humanity. As a philosopher he sets even more severe standards for himself. His style in the Epistles is in general dry, laconic, and oracular.[103] It is not this Apollonius nor Damis who contributed to the *Life* the rich overlay of interest in the arts : rather it was Philostratus, the author of the εἰκόνες.

This study of Philostratus' *Life of Apollonius of Tyana* has made clear its type and its affiliations. It is a Greek romance of a new type, the historical-philosophical. Possibly its original prototype was Xenophon's *Cyropaedia,* for Xenophon's "Greek was the favourite model of his particular school." [104] And as Xenophon in this *Education of Cyrus* was presenting under the history of Cyrus

99 II. 20.
100 V. 5.
101 II. 22 ; VI. 10.
102 Philostratus, *The Life of Apollonius of Tyana* in *The Loeb Classical Library,* New York, 1926, II. 408–81.
103 E. Meyer, *op. cit.,* pp. 405–14.
104 J. S. Phillimore, *op. cit.,* I. xix.

the Great a picture of the ideal ἀρχικὸς ἀνήρ, the man fit to rule, and the best form of government, so Philostratus is presenting in the person of Apollonius of Tyana the θεῖος ἀνήρ, the philosopher who is a little lower than the gods and the best way of life.[105]   Military campaigns demonstrate the abilities of Cyrus, philosophical discourses the spiritual qualities of Apollonius.   Both romances achieve a new fusion of Oriental and Occidental thought : Xenophon's in Persian and Spartan conceptions of the ideal king-ruler ; Philostratus' in Brahman and Pythagorean demonstrations of the transcendental powers of the divine sage.   But while the *Cyropaedia* was an antecedent of the Greek love romances in its beautiful inset story of the loves of Panthea and Abradatas,[106] the *Life* of the ascetic Pythagorean displayed no interest in the relation between the sexes.

In plot the *Life of Apollonius of Tyana* owed much to the Greek tales of travel (the lost *The Wonderful Things beyond Thule* of Antonius Diogenes and others) which Lucian satirized so brilliantly in his *True History*.   And, as in these old stories of adventure, geography and chronology were less important to Philostratus than the marvels he saw and the pursuit of his quest.   In Philostratus just as in the Greek love romances the elements of adventure and religion are present.   But adventures are side-lines for the single aim of the attainment of philosophical knowledge.   Religions are fused into a pantheism that embraces all gods.   Temples are visited for reform of rituals.   And love between man and woman is superseded by communion of a sage with the one and only god. The disciples of the sage approach god through their devotion to their Master, the divine man, the human savior.

---

[105] Gilbert Murray, *A History of Ancient Greek Literature*, New York, 1908, pp. 317, 322-23.

[106] E. H. Haight, *Essays on Ancient Fiction*, New York, 1936, pp. 22-29.

In his technique, Philostratus, learned Sophist that he was, uses all the various devices of the Greek love romances : conversation, purple patches of descriptions, anecdotes ; documentary evidence of letters and inscriptions ; a plentiful introduction of historical personages ; prison scenes ; court-room scenes with their rhetorical speeches ; magical effluvia of dreams, miracles, and epiphanies. And all the training of the rhetorician must contribute its part.

"To realize the true sophistic manner," writes Phillimore,[107] "there must be much Hellenizing : plenty of history, rhetorically sauced ; plenty of archaeology. Apollonius (who was probably of Hittite or Amorite stock, if in fact he was descended from the founders of Tyana) must be made all that is most Greek, an Atticist but without pedantry, donnish yet modish ; his talk enriched with Homeric quotations, and brilliantly freaked with allusive poeticisms. It was a theme on which the sophists' commonplace book might be emptied out. There was room for many a neat page on mythology, aesthetics, and literature. Philostratus has by him a little thing on Flute-playing : put this into Apollonius' mouth, and the futility of the dialogue is rather less apparent (V. 21). Every schoolboy would be gratified and encouraged when he found Apollonius showing knowledge of his Demosthenes' *de Corona*. Prodicus' celebrated Apologue must serve as a model for a similar *Apollonius' Choice*. Topical *Dialexeis* must be introduced at suitable points : a Sermon in prison, a Sermon on Facing Tyrants, &c., &c., the conventional debate on the Merits of a Republic compared with a Monarchy, and above all, the centerpiece of the fabric, Philostratus' 'benefit' performance, a grand scholastic μελέτη, Apollonius' Apologia before Domitian.' "

The elements of magic and of theurgy in Philostratus make him more closely affiliated with the Latin novelist Apuleius than with the writers of the Greek love romances. Both Apuleius and Apollonius had to defend themselves in court against charges of practising magic and each composed his own *Apologia*. Both were scholars of broad learning and had travelled widely. Both had

[107] J. S. Phillimore, *op. cit.*, I. lxxiii–lxxiv.

the reputation of being philosophers : Apuleius a Pla-
tonist, Apollonius a Pythagorean. Both Apuleius and
Philostratus claimed to base their romances on earlier
writings : Apuleius on a certain Greek tale (perhaps
Λούκιος ἢ ὄνος), Philostratus on Damis' memoirs of Apollonius. "Both have much to say of transformations, wizards, demons, and the occult." [108] Beyond all that, both
in their romances were writing a sort of Pilgrim's Progress
of a valiant hero who, assailed by the various temptations
of life and tested by various adventures, was seeking the
Holy Grail of a meaning for life itself. Lucius satisfied
his quest in the religion of Isis. Apollonius found his
salvation in a synthesis of the Brahman and the Pythagorean philosophers.

Perhaps the most mooted of all questions concerning
the *Life of Apollonius of Tyana* is its relation to Christianity. To be sure, Philostratus never mentions Christ
or the Christians, but that has not prevented scholars
since the time of the early church fathers from stating that
he presents his hero as a rival of Christ. It is noteworthy
that this exaltation of Apollonius as a rival of Christ does
not appear in ancient writers between the time of Apollonius and Philostratus, nor does it gain prominence soon
after the publication of Philostratus' book. Lucian, the
earliest author to allude to Apollonius, speaks of him as
a magician.[109] Dio Cassius refers to his second sight at
the time of Domitian's death and to Caracalla's worship of
him, but regards him as a sorcerer.[110] Alexander Severus
honored him in his Lararium with Christ, Abraham, and
Orpheus.[111]

It was in the time of Diocletian that a provincial governor, Hierocles, wrote a book "to show that Apollonius

[108] Lynn Thorndike, *op. cit.,* I.
242–43.
[109] Lucian, *Alexander,* 5.
[110] Dio Cassius, *Epit.* LXVII. 17,
18 ; LXXVII. 18, 4.
[111] *Script. Hist. Aug. Alex.* 29.

had been as great a sage, as remarkable a worker of miracles, and as potent an exorcist as Jesus Christ." [112] The
Christian historian Eusebius wrote a treatise in answer to
Hierocles "Against the Life of Apollonius of Tyana written by Philostratus, occasioned by the parallel drawn by
Hierocles between him and Christ." [113] Eusebius points
out that no anti-Christian writer before Hierocles had
claimed that Apollonius was a rival of Christ.   While ad-
mitting Apollonius' powers, he claims that his miracles
were wrought by the help of evil spirits, demons.   And he
attacks Philostratus by analyzing the inconsistencies in
the *Life*.

Few if any scholars would now claim that Philostratus
wrote his book to present his hero as a rival of Christ.[114]
There exist, of course, parallelisms between the lives of
Apollonius and Jesus, but these could be drawn between
the lives of Apollonius and Saint Paul as well.[115]   Philostratus seems almost certainly to have known the New
Testament and certain Apocryphal *Acta,*[116] which I
have shown to be Christian Greek Romances.   But
farther than these allusions borrowings cannot be sub-
stantiated.[117]   Philostratus like other writers of the early
Empire simply reflects the general belief in demonology
and wonder-working in the age.[118]   His originality did
not lie in writing a romance about a real person, for
Xenophon had written the *Cyropaedia,* and probably before Philostratus' time there existed some early version
of *The History of Alexander the Great.*   But with full
knowledge of Xenophon's romantic biography of Cyrus

[112] F. C. Conybeare, in *Philostratus,*
op. cit., I. xii.

[113] *Ibid.,* II. 485.

[114] A. Chassang, *op. cit.,* pp. xii–
xiii.

[115] B. L. Gildersleeve, *op. cit.,* 294–
96.

[116] J. S. Phillimore, *op. cit.,* I.
lxxvi–vii.

[117] B. L. Gildersleeve, *op. cit.,* p.
293.

[118] A. Chassang, *op. cit.,* pp. 462–65.

the Elder as the ideal ruler, of the Greek novels of war and adventure, of the Greek love romances, of the *controversiae* and the *suasoriae* of the rhetorical schools and of the Christian *Acta* with a saint for the hero, Philostratus chose to present a θεῖος ἀνήρ, a divine sage, a Pythagorean philosopher, as the center of his story. To make the life of his hero interesting and to promulgate his philosophy he uses every device of the Greek and Latin novels of the Second and Third Centuries. And the credulity, the discourses, the aspirations of his characters belong as much to all the first three centuries of the Empire as to the age of the Severi. Philostratus has written out of the restless cravings of that time another romance to help men escape from the burden of their fears to life's fairer possibilities.

V

APULEIUS AND BOCCACCIO

"THE greatest story-teller in the world ! Does that seem a hard saying ? But by what other title shall we greet the author of the Decameron ? . . . The greatest work of the fourteenth century, as the *Divine Comedy* had been of the thirteenth, the *Decameron* sums up and reflects its period altogether impersonally." [1]

So may Edward Hutton introduce to us Giovanni Boc-caccio. By one of those striking literary affinities which seem to substantiate the doctrine of transmigration of souls the spirit of Apuleius of Madaura seems rein-carnated in Boccaccio of Certaldo. Certainly the Ro-man's art of narration reappears for the first time in full flower in the Florentine after a gap of twelve centuries. Rich material is available for comparing the technique of the two story-tellers, for in the *Decameron* Boccaccio re-told in Italian two novelle from Apuleius' *Metamor-phoses* and in his *De Genealogiis Deorum* he rewrote in Latin Apuleius' story of Cupid and Psyche and attempted a philosophical interpretation of it. In two of his great-est works, then, one the famous collection of stories in the Italian vernacular, the other the encyclopedic history of mythology in Latin, Boccaccio himself furnishes us proof of his close affinity to the greatest ancient novelist.

Boccaccio's admiration for Apuleius is further attested

---

[1] Edward Hutton, *Giovanni Boccaccio,* London and New York, 1910, p. 291.

by the existence of his own copy of Apuleius, all written in his own hand,[2] and by his several references to his works.[3]   Boccaccio not only mentions and uses the *Metamorphoses* "qui vulgariori vocabulo Asinus aureus appellatur," [4] but he recognizes Apuleius as a philosopher of no slight prestige, "non mediocris auctoritatis philosophus," [5] and quotes the *De Mundo*,[6] the *De Dogmate Platonis*,[7] and the *Asclepius*.[8]   Perhaps then partly through Apuleius, the *Platonicus nobilis* of Saint Augustine, Boccaccio became impregnated with that neo-Platonism which was to color his interpretations of mythology.   Certainly his other debts to Apuleius were great. I wish to portray them as they appear in the *Decameron* and in *The Genealogy of the Gods*.

The plots of Apuleius' and Boccaccio's novels are alike in being designed as frames for the set of a series of disconnected novelle or short stories, but they are as utterly dissimilar in pattern as the times in which the authors wrote.   Apuleius in the Second Century of our era, when the Roman Empire had conquered the Mediterranean world, expressed in a picaresque novel the quest of a roving hero for some philosophical meaning (in magic, the old religion, the new Oriental cults) for his individual life.   Boccaccio in the Fourteenth Century in plague-ridden Florence with no further purpose than entertainment produced one hundred tales which reflected the life of his time with all its varied characters in all its amorality.

Apuleius' plot is cinematic in rapidity of change of scene and in variety of scenes.   His hero Lucius, unfor-

2 Oskar Hecker, *Boccaccio-Funde*, Brunswick, 1901, pp. 34–35. The manuscript is in the Laurentian Library, Plut. 54, Nr 32.

3 Attilio Hortis, *Studj sulle opere latine del Boccaccio*, Trieste, 1879, pp. 455–56.

4 *De Gen. Deor.*, V. c. 22.
5 *De Gen. Deor.*, I. c. 5.
6 *De Gen. Deor.*, I. c. 5.
7 *De Gen. Deor.*, I. c. 15.
8 *De Gen. Deor.*, III. c. 20.

tunately changed into an ass when dabbling in magic rites, wanders up and down the world meeting strange adventures until at last he finds salvation and retransformation to man's shape through the mercy of the goddess Isis. Boccaccio's plot is static in its placement of a group of ten young nobles (seven ladies, three gentlemen) in a great house-party of ten days at first one, then a second villa outside Florence where in the heat of the day they forget the menacing horror of swift-coming death in telling stories to each other. But dissimilar as are the motivation and the designs of the plot the art of narration in the individual stories shows many of the same characteristics.

The sources of Boccaccio's novelle are manifold and not always easily traceable,[9] "Egyptian, Arabian, Persian, and French" Hutton says. "Certainly to the Contes and Fabliaux of Northern France a third part of the *Decameron* may be traced, much too to Indian and Persian sources, and a little to the *Gesta Romanorum*." But "he has made the tales his own." [10]

In discussing the functions of story-telling in *The Genealogy of the Gods* Boccaccio recognized what today is called "escape literature" and he illustrated his point by a reference to Apuleius :

"Fiction has, in some cases, sufficed to lift the oppressive weight of adversity and furnish consolation, as appears in Lucius Apuleius ; he tells how the highborn maiden Charis, while bewailing her unhappy condition as captive among thieves, was in some degree restored through hearing from an old woman the charming story of Psyche." [11]

9 A. Bartoli, *I precursori del Boccaccio*, Firenze, 1876 ; M. Landau, *Die Quellen des Dekameron*, Stuttgart, 1884 ; L. Cappelletti, *Osservazioni e notizie sulle fonti del Decamerone*, Livorno, 1891 ; G. Gröber, *Ueber die Quellen von Boccaccios Dekameron*, Strasbourg, 1913.

10 E. Hutton, *op. cit.*, p. 304.
11 *De Gen. Deor.*, XIV. 9. The translations of passages from the Preface and Books XIV and XV of the *De Gen. Deor.*, are from Charles G. Osgood, *Boccaccio on Poetry*, Princeton, 1930.

That sentence might be written on the fly-leaf of the *Decameron,* for its stories were told to bring to ten young people forgetfulness of the terrible plague which in the year 1348 had carried off over one hundred thousand of the inhabitants of their native city, Florence. The preface of the *Decameron* describes the awful scenes within Florence itself, the stench of the unburied dead, the immorality of the reckless living. And in contrast, the beauty of the country setting for the story-telling is over and over again described : the fair, orderly villa with its halls full of flowers ; the spacious grounds, where on the green grass under the shade of trees in the mingled music of nightingales and waterfalls the young people at the order of the Ruler of the Day enlivened each other by their tales. In such a set for such a company with such an object it was natural that the story-tellers vied with each other in excursions into wit, satire, and eroticism. The two stories taken over bodily from Apuleius' *Metamorphoses* illustrate all these three types.[12] Apuleius' story of "The Lover hid in the Cask" is one of those Milesian tales which he engrafted in the *Metamorphoses* upon the simpler narrative of Λούκιος ἢ ὄνος, as we see it at least in the extant epitome.[13] This salacious tale was such a favorite that it was re-told many times.

"Morlini, a Neapolitan doctor of laws of the Sixteenth Century, narrated it in Latin in his book of short stories (*Novella* 35) with a moral attached at the end : 'Novella indicat neminem fraudibus mulierum posse resistere.' La Fontaine in the Seventeenth Century re-wrote it in a delicious French poem of seventy-four lines, 'Le Cuvier,' beginning and ending with the verse ; 'Soyez amant, vous serez inventif.' And 'Le Cuvier' inspired three comic operas in France as well as an English 'musical entertainment,' all in the Eighteenth Century."[14]

[12] *Decameron,* VII. 2 = *Met.* IX. 4–7 ; *Decameron,* V. 10 = *Met.* IX. 22–28.

[13] *Met.* IX. 4–7 = *Dec.* VII. 2.
[14] E. H. Haight, *Apuleius and His Influence,* New York, 1927, p. 114.

This very short story, which covers only three pages of Latin in the Loeb edition of the *Metamorphoses* and four of Italian in the complete Hoepli *Decameron,* is a comedy of low life on the eternal triangle of wanton wife, deceived husband, ingenious lover.   In Apuleius, the narrator is Lucius, the Ass-Man ; in Boccaccio the narrator is Filostrato, the liveliest of the three young nobles in the party.   Lucius' introduction is the briefest possible, "lepidam de adulterio cuiusdam pauperis fabulam." Filostrato begins with a long satirical flourish about what is good for the gander is good for the goose, or the tables may be turned ; women as well as men are deceivers, if not ever, then often !

Both Apuleius and Boccaccio etch sharply the characterizations of the three actors in the story, though in Apuleius they have no names.   Boccaccio calls the wife Peronella, the husband Avorio, and the lover Giannello Strignario. Apuleius likewise does not name the town in which the episode occurred.   Boccaccio places it appropriately in Naples, where he spent the gay days of his youth.   In each the husband is a worker : a smith, a stone-cutter. The wife adds to the family's small income by spinning at home, but she is a light nature, "postrema lascivia famigerabilis," "una bella e vaga giovanetta."   The husband is hard-working and stupid.

The episode is the same in both authors.   When the husband went out to work, the lover came in to play, but one day the husband came home unexpectedly early.   On finding the door locked he happily reflected on his wife's careful virtue and made known his presence by a whistle and a knock.   The wife hid her lover in an empty cask with an excited speech to him (not in Apuleius), then opened the door.

In both Apuleius and Boccaccio the rest of the story is

told by lively conversation, but Boccaccio gives us much more of it. The Latin wife upbraids her husband for his early return with empty hands, bearing no food for the table, while she spins all night and all day to get enough oil for their lamp. The wife next door has lovers and food and wine and fun ! What is the good of virtue ? All this and curses too the Italian wife repeats. The horrified husband in each case is apologetic and soothing. The excuse of the Latin husband is that his master had business in the Forum and dismissed his workers ; of the Italian that it is the festival of San Galeone when no one works. In spite of that each husband proudly announces that he is provident, for he has sold their old cask for five pieces of money. The wife instantly seeing a way of escape from her predicament boasts that she a stay-at-home has just found a purchaser who will pay seven coins, in fact at this moment he is inside the cask inspecting it. The lover who has been all ears hereupon makes an entrance from the cask, pretends not to know who the husband is, and declares the cask is so filthy that it must be cleaned before he can see whether it is sound enough to purchase. The delighted simpleton of a husband at once gets a light and goes into the cask to scrape it. His wife directs the cleaning, putting her head and one arm inside the opening. While she is stretched over the cask, the lover outside reassumes his interrupted sport with her as, says Boccaccio, the unbridled Parthian horses in the meadows assail the mares. The work of both husband and lover is finished simultaneously. The lover pays his seven coins. The husband carries the cask home for him ! .

Boccaccio has made almost a translation of Apuleius' tale. Yet by giving Italian names to city and persons, by expanding the introduction with ironic satire, by enlarg-

ing the conversation with a flood of Italian vituperation
he has written what seems a completely contemporary
Italian story.

The other story which Boccaccio took from Apuleius,
the story of the baker's wife, is retold by him in a very
different way.[15] Apuleius' story is another Milesian tale,
but it is treated much more elaborately than the story of
the smith's wife. He gives a full description of the baker's mill, and the conditions there. A long denunciatory
sketch of the baker's wife sets her character before she begins to act and talk. Two inset stories, one of the sandals
under the bed, one of the fuller's wife, illustrate and di-
versify the main theme, the frailty of woman's virtue.
And the atmosphere of the whole narrative changes from
utmost realism in the preliminary description of the tor-
ture of slaves and beasts in the mill to a mirage of magic
in which the wicked wife, a witch, and a ghost cause the
baker's death. Boccaccio has simplified and shortened
by omitting both the realistic picture at the beginning
and the murder by the ghost at the end, by omitting too
the whole inset story of the sandals under the bed. Moreover, his character-drawing does not follow closely
Apuleius' technique.

The narrator in Apuleius is again Lucius, the ass. In
Boccaccio another one of the young men, Dioneo, tells
the ribald tale. Apuleius puts the scene in "the next
village," Boccaccio in Perugia. Apuleius does not give
names to his characters except in the story of the sandals
under the bed. Boccaccio calls the husband Pietro di
Vinciolo and his friend Ercolano, but does not give names
to the two wives, to the lover, or to the old bawd. The
preliminary characterizations of the story are different.
Lucius the ass calls it "fabulam . . . bonam prae ceteris

15 *Met.* IX. 10–31 = *Dec.* V. 10.

suavem," while Dioneo says that, of course, men laugh more over *cattive cose* than over *buone opere,* but his hearers are free to gather the roses in his garden of humanity and leave the thorns, if only they feel compassion for mankind.

Lucius the ass full of moral indignation gives a vituperative character-sketch of the baker's wife, "the most pestilent woman in all the world" into whose heart had flowed all the evils in the world "as into some filthy privy." [16] Boccaccio is content with a brief label of wantonness for the woman and lets her reveal her own character by soliloquy, speeches, and actions. These methods of characterization are reversed by the two authors in the case of the old bawd. In Apuleius she betrays her corruption by her advice to the fuller's wife and by the story she tells her about Philesitherus (the sandals under the bed), a new lover whom she proposes for her. In Boccaccio on the contrary the bawd's character is revealed in a long, shameless, ironic speech about women and the inset story about Philesitherus is omitted. The lover introduced is simply the handsomest youth in Perugia.

In both the Latin and the Italian the main episode is the same : when the baker returns early from dining at the fuller's, the baker's wife conceals her lover (in Apuleius in a flour bin, in Boccaccio in a chicken-coop). The husband to explain his early return relates the story of the fuller's wife : how her lover, who was hidden in a sulphur-vat where clothes were cleaned, overcome by the fumes betrayed himself by sneezing. The baker's wife curses the fuller's wife and says that all such women for their corruption should be burned alive. Boccaccio makes the baker's wife's hypocrisy more comic by having her

---

[16] The translations are from *Apuleius, the Golden Ass,* by W. Adlington, revised by S. Gaselee in *The Loeb Classical Library,* New York, 1928.

reel off a long, direct speech of horrified virtue. She is exposed in both novels by an ass, for in Apuleius Lucius in righteous indignation steps purposely on the fingers of her lover which were protruding from the flour-bin so the lover screams, and in Boccaccio a stray ass stabled near the room, while roaming in search of water, accidentally steps on the fingers of the lover protruding from the chicken-coop.

Here the treatment of the dénouement is different. In Apuleius, the husband in a few ironic, jesting words, tells the young man that he will do him no harm, but simply will share his wife's pleasure in him, since they have always lived in harmony, enjoying the same diversions. The next morning the husband has the youth flogged, upbraiding him for his adultery and divorces his wife. Boccaccio complicates the plot by making the discovered lover the lad, for love of whom the baker had deserted his wife, and he inserts a long, frank, ironic conversation between husband and wife on each other's sins. Boccaccio makes the cuckold husband insist on having a dinner-party *à trois* before he takes his vengeance. Boccaccio only hints what the vengeance is and warns the dear ladies that turn about is fair play. His story stops suddenly there.

In Apuleius the baker's wife, true to Lucius' description of her evil machinations, finds a witch woman and gives her a commission either to restore her husband to her or destroy him. When the witch by all her enchantments cannot achieve the first, she destroys the baker by sending to him the ghost of a woman who had met a violent death, and this ghost contrives that the baker should hang himself. The whole story of this witchcraft is revealed by the baker's ghost who with a rope around his neck appears at night to his married daughter in the next village and tells her all the wickedness of her step-mother.

Apuleius' story of the baker's wife is the longest and most elaborate of his Milesian tales and illustrates all the varied technique of his art of narration : the advantage of the ironic man-ass narrator, the exciting contrasts of realism and super-realism in the atmosphere of the set, the character-drawing through description, conversation, and comment, the accumulative force of three stories on the one theme of woman's frailty. Boccaccio, for his purpose of a very short story purporting to be one of ten told orally on a hot afternoon for entertainment, has condensed and simplified Apuleius to a single Italian episode full of spice, naughtiness, and merriment.

Boccaccio's relation to Apuleius appears in a very different aspect in *The Genealogy of the Gods*. This encyclopedia of mythology, begun probably when Boccaccio was thirty and continued for about thirty years, was the work of Boccaccio the scholar, not of Boccaccio the raconteur. It was inspired by Petrarch, his adored friend and master, who valued research written in Latin far above stories in the vulgar tongue. It was commissioned, if we may take Boccaccio's preface as true, by King Hugo of Cyprus, who laid upon the young writer the hard task of collecting, ordering, and interpreting all the myths of the Gentile gods. But the Boccaccio of the *Decameron* and the Boccaccio of the *Genealogy* are "one and the same man" as Osgood says : [17]

"One cannot remind oneself too often that Boccaccio's scholarship and his art were but projections of the same powers of his mind, and that his humanistic Latin prose works come unmistakably from the hand of a poet."

"Boccaccio speaks, then, at once as poet, critic and scholar. Nor does he from time to time exchange one function for another, but

[17] C. G. Osgood, *op. cit.,* pp. xi and xvi.

all three powers of his mind are coactive throughout his discussion, if indeed they are not really one and single."

In the various prefaces to the fifteen books of the *Genealogy* as well as sometimes in the text itself, Boccaccio talks to his readers about the nature of his work, the functions and the art of story-telling, and the interpretation of the myths. A summary of these self-revealing comments will be a fitting prelude to his use of Apuleius' story of Cupid and Psyche.

Both at the beginning and at the end of the *Genealogy* Boccaccio explains the nature of his work. His own words in the conclusion of Book XV make clear his conception of it :

"I have employed such skill as I have in recounting the traditionary genealogy of the Gentile gods and their posterity ; these I have ascertained with wide research and set down in order. In obedience to your command, I have according to my ability added interpretation to the myths, both derived from the ancients and from my own slender intellect." [18]

Research, arrangement, and interpretation were then no less his aims than his achievement.

The great story-teller has also much to say about the functions of story-telling. Fiction has quelled passions, refreshed worn spirits by diversion, comforted the oppressed, stimulated the dull.[19] And stories have been the ornament of many forms of literature besides poetry, even of orators.[20] For all these reasons, the art of story-telling must be as free and self-sufficient as the painter's

[18] The Latin text used is that of O. Hecker, *Boccaccio-Funde,* Brunswick, 1902 ; the translations of the prefaces and Books XIV and XV are from C. G. Osgood, *Boccaccio on Poetry,* Princeton, 1932. *De Gen. Deor.,* XV. *Conclusio.* O. Hecker, *op. cit.,* p. 297 ; C. G. Osgood, *op. cit.,* pp. 140–41.

[19] *De Gen. Deor.,* XIV. 9 ; O. Hecker, *op. cit.,* p. 218 ; C. G. Osgood, *op. cit.,* pp. 50–51.

[20] *De Gen. Deor.,* XV. 1 ; O. Hecker, *op. cit.,* pp. 263–64 ; C. G. Osgood, *op. cit.,* p. 104.

art. The tale must be told for itself and never criticized
as vicious for "sin consists not in the knowledge of evil,
but in the act." [21]   And for such free art of narration,
brevity is all important : there must be no prolixity to
dull the brilliance of the legend ; no verbosity to quench
the reader's imagination, which must by its response enrich each tale told.[22]

Author and reader together must rediscover the meaning, the philosophy in the myth, for

"there was never a maundering old woman, sitting with others
late of a winter's night at the home fireside, making up tales of
Hell, the fates, ghosts, and the like — much of it pure invention —
that she did not feel beneath the surface of her tale, as far as her
limited mind allowed, at least some meaning — sometimes ridic-
ulous no doubt — with which she tries to scare the little ones, or
divert the young ladies, or amuse the old, or at least show the power
of fortune." [23]

Boccaccio believing devoutly in the hidden meaning
of the myths perceived clearly all the pitfalls in the path
of the elucidator.   Hence he craves indulgence from his
patron and from his reader for the imperfections of his
work :

"Though the learned more often perceive that which escapes the
unlearned, yet it sometimes happens that an unlearned man may
see what the learned have overlooked.   I am human, and it is no
new and strange thing for a human being to err." [24]

Boccaccio himself gives the most disarming comment
on the difficulty of his task :

"Who in our day can penetrate the hearts of the Ancients ?
Who can bring to light and life again minds long since removed

[21] *De Gen. Deor.*, XIV. 18; O.
Hecker, *op. cit.*, p. 245 ; C. G. Osgood,
op. cit., pp. 82–83.
   [22] *De Gen. Deor.*, XV. 12 ; O.
Hecker, *op. cit.*, pp. 291–92 ; C. G. Osgood, *op. cit.*, pp. 135–36.

[23] *De Gen. Deor.*, XIV. 10 ; O.
Hecker, *op. cit.*, p. 221 ; C. G. Osgood,
op. cit., pp. 50–51.
   [24] *De Gen. Deor.*, XV. 4 ; O.
Hecker, *op. cit.*, p. 267 ; C. G. Osgood,
op. cit., p. 109.

in death ?   Who can elicit their meaning ?   A divine task that —
not human !" [25]

How sympathetically Boccaccio approached "the heart
of the ancients" may be seen from his rendering of
Apuleius' famous story of Cupid and Psyche.   Since the
Latin text is not available, as far as I know, in a modern
edition, I present here a complete translation of Boccaccio's rendering and interpretation.   The edition used is
the Vassar incunabulum, Venice, 1497.[26]   The Latin is
printed in Appendix I.   With the text and translation
before us it will be possible to discuss adequately Boccaccio's treatment.

Boccaccio, *De Genealogiis Deorum,* Venice, 1497.
V. 22, *De Psyche. XV. Apollinis filia.*
On Psyche, the daughter of Apollo

Psyche as Martianus Capella says,[27] in the book which
he wrote about the marriage of Mercury and Philologia,
was the daughter of Apollo and Endelichia.   About her
Lucius Apuleius in the book of the *Metamorphoses* which
in more vulgar parlance is called the *Golden Ass* tells a
somewhat longer story that runs like this.[28]   Once upon
a time there were a king and a queen who had three daughters.   Although the two older of these were handsome,
the younger, whose name was Psyche, so far surpassed

[25] *De Gen. Deor., Prohemium* ; O.
Hecker, *op. cit.,* pp. 169–70 ; C. G.
Osgood, *op. cit.,* p. 11.
[26] Incunabula. — Boccaccio. Gene-
ologia deorum gentilium (A 1 imper-
fect) . . . boccatii, cum demonstra-
tionibus in formis arborum designatis.
Eiusdem de montibus et silvis, de fon-
tibus, lacubus et fluminibus ac etiam
de stagnis et paludibus, nec non et de
maribus seu diversis maris nominibus,
printed in Roman letter, 63 long lines
to a page (folios A 1 to A 6 defective
taking away a quarter of the page in
each case, these 11. comprise the table, the work itself, apart from the
table being in good order), folio, bds.,
*Impressum Venetiis per me Man-
fredum de Strevo De Monteferrato,
MCCCCXCVII.,* Venice, 1497 £ 4 4 s
   In Hain, 3324 ; and Proctor, 5367.
For a full description of another copy
of this edition see A. Hortis, *op. cit.,*
p. 780, no. XIX.
[27] I. 7.
[28] Met. IV. 28–VI. 24.

other mortal maids in beauty that she not only won the admiration of those who beheld her, but in ignorant souls she inspired by the miracle of the fact a belief that she was Venus, who had come down to earth.   Now the fame of her unseen beauty, which spread far and wide, brought about that not only citizens but strangers came to look upon Venus and to honor her with sacrifices.   The temples of the true Venus were deserted.   Venus indignant at this and angered at Psyche ordered her son Cupid to inflame the girl with ardent love for a man of low estate. Meanwhile Psyche's father consulted Apollo of Miletus about the marriage of the maid.   Apollo answered that he should place her on a mountain-top and there the girl would find a husband of divine descent, really a terrible serpent.   Psyche's parents overcome by this oracle, with the whole state weeping and mourning, escorted the girl to the predestined peak and left her there alone.   Although she was distressed by the solitude and by dread of her future husband all unknown, still she did not have to wait long.   For kind Zephyr came and lifting her on gentle breath bore her to a flowery mead, where he lightened her suffering with sleep for a time.   Arising she beheld a grove fair to see and a spring with silver jets of water and a palace not merely royal but divine, adorned with great wealth.   When she had entered it and found mighty treasures unguarded and had marvelled at them greatly, she heard incorporeal voices of servants and, when she went into the bath, the invisible creatures assisted her with devoted care.   Then a dinner of rich foods fit for the gods was served her.   Finally she entered the bedroom and ascended the marriage bed.   In her sleep her husband came and made her his wife and at dawn departed without having been seen.   This happened over and over and was a great comfort to Psyche.   Now her sisters hav-

ing heard of the sad fate of Psyche went from their husbands' homes to their mourning parents and with them
bewailed the ill-fated marriage of their sister.   But Cupid,
foreseeing what was being prepared for Psyche through
the envy of her sisters, admonished her that she should not
heed their tears at all nor be devoted and credulous to her
own destruction.   After Psyche had promised this, she
began to lament her lot as a captive both because she could
not see her sisters and because she could not talk with
them.   When Cupid came and argued with her, she won
him by her prayers to let her talk with them and to bid
Zephyr to waft them to her on a gentle breeze.   Cupid
granted also that after Zephyr had done this, Psyche might
let them carry away whatever treasures they wished, but
he urged that in no particular should she trust their advice
nor on the counsel of anyone desire to see his face.   Now
at home the sisters lamented for Psyche.   Then they
ascended the mountain and when their shrill wailing was
renewed, Psyche heard them and comforted them with a
few words.   Finally, at the order of Psyche Zephyr bore
them down to a fair vale.   There Psyche received them
with happy greetings and showed them all her treasures.
And since her sisters were envious of these, they urged
with all their might that she try to see her husband.
Psyche sent them away with gifts ; then, credulous girl,
she prepared a razor and hid a lamp under a jar, for she
was resolved when night came on, to see what sort of a
creature slept with her, resolved too, if his aspect con-
formed to her sister's words, to slay him.   Then in the
usual way Cupid came to bed and went to sleep.   But
Psyche, when the lamp was uncovered, saw that her bed-
fellow was a youth of marvellous beauty, adorned with
swift wings, and near his feet were bow and quiver packed
with arrows.   One of these the amazed Psyche drew forth

to try the edge, and so pressed it on her finger that a little blood spurted from the wound. Because of this she was inflamed with mad love for the sleeping god. While she gazed on him in rapture, a little ember from the lamp fell on his right shoulder. Awakened by the burn Cupid suddenly flew away. But Psyche, as she began to cling to his leg and stoutly clutched it, was borne by him through the air so long that finally worn out she loosened her hold and fell. Cupid, however, flying up into a cypress near, in a long complaint denounced her, and condemned himself because, when sent by his mother to inflame her with love for a man of low estate, he himself had wounded himself on account of her beauty. Then off he flew. Psyche, distressed over the loss of her husband, wished to die. At least by deceit she destroyed her sisters, through whose counsels she had come to grief, by making them fall over a precipice. Then she was violently upbraided by Venus and tortured by blows from her servants. At the order of Venus she was involved in tasks impossible for a mortal. But aided by the work of her lover she came through unconquered, and at last by his prayers to Jupiter it came about that she won Venus' favor ; she was taken up to heaven and lived in eternal and happy wedlock with Cupid. To him she bore a child, Joy.

Most noble king, if we should wish to explain in detail the sense of this very great story, the work would fill a huge book. And so it must be sufficient to state with a few of the attending circumstances why Psyche is called the daughter of Apollo and Endelichia, who her sisters are, and why she is said to be the wife of Cupid. Now Psyche is interpreted as the soul. She, moreover, is said to be the daughter of Apollo, that is of the sun, that god forsooth who is the true light of the world, for the crea-

tion of the thinking soul belongs to no other power but
god. Endelichia, moreover, as Calcidius on the *Timaeus*
of Plato remarks, is interpreted as the perfect age whose
daughter is said to be the truly rational soul because even
in the womb of her mother we receive her from the father of light. Nevertheless, her works do not appear except in the perfect age since we are shaped even up to the
perfect age rather by a certain natural instinct than by
rational judgment. But in the perfect age we begin to
act from reason. So she is well named the daughter of
Apollo and Endelichia. She has two sisters who are older,
not because they were born first, but because they use
their power first. Of these one is called the nutritive
faculty, but the other the sensitive faculty and these are
not souls as some have proclaimed, but they are functions of the soul. And so Psyche is said to be the younger,
because long before her the nutritive faculty is granted
to the foetus and afterwards in the course of time the
sensitive faculty. At last, moreover, reason is granted
to this Psyche. Now because they are first in action, they
are said to be the first to be wed, while Psyche is saved
for this rational divine offspring, that is noble love or
god himself. To joy with him she is borne down by
Zephyr, that is by the breath of life which is holy, and
she is married. Cupid forbids his wife to desire to see
him unless she wishes to lose him. This means she
should not wish to have a vision of his immortality, of
the beginnings of the world, of the omnipotent, for reasons which are known to himself alone. For as often as
we mortals investigate such matters, we destroy him, nay
more our very selves, by turning aside from the straight
road. The sisters, however, sometimes arrive even at
the first goal of Psyche's joys and from her treasures they
carry away as much as those do who live in reason. The

nutritive faculty does her work better. And the virtues of the sensitive faculty are brighter and they endure longer. They, of course, envy their sister, for it is not at all strange that sensation is at variance with reason, and when they cannot persuade her by blandishments to look upon her husband, that is, to wish to see by natural reason what she loves and not to know it by faith, they attempt to induce her by horrors, declaring that he is a huge serpent and that he will devour her. And, indeed, as often as sensation attempts to lull reason to rest and to display to the soul a vision even of things known by reason, this would happen, that not only are the delights of sensation removed, but enormous toils and untimely sufferings are added and finally there follows implacable retribution. The soul, moreover, while without wisdom, puts confidence in such demonstrations, and desires to see what is denied and is ready to die if beauty does not appear in answer to her prayer. She sees the most fair form of her husband, that is, the outer works of god. She cannot see the beauty, that is, the divinity, because no one ever sees god. And with the little hot ember she hurts and wounds him, that is, on account of proud desire, through which she becomes disobedient, and trusting sensation she loses the blessing of contemplation. And so she is separated from the marriage with god. At last penitent and loving she accomplishes the destruction of her relatives by her cleverness and so checks them that they have no power against reason. Then purified by toils and sufferings, freed from haughty pride and disobedience, she again finds the blessing of joy and contemplation in god, and she gives herself to him forever, until having put aside mortality she is borne away to immortal glory. There, one with love, she gives birth to Joy, that is eternal delight and happiness.

Boccaccio, *De Genealogiis Deorum,* Venice, 1497.
IX. 4, *De Cupidine primo Martis filio qui genuit Voluptatem.*

On Cupid, first son of Mars, who was the father of Joy

Cupid, as Tullius says in his book *On the Nature of the
Gods,*[29] was the son of Mars and Venus.   Foolish persons,
both ancient and modern, wish him to be a god of great
power.   This is clear from the poem of Seneca the writer
of tragedies, who said of him in the tragedy *Hippolytus* : [30]

"And he orders the gods above having left heaven to
inhabit earth in disguise.   Phoebus as the shepherd of
the Thessalian herd tended cattle, and having laid aside
his plectrum called the bulls by Pan's pipes.   How often
the very god who rules heaven and the clouds put on
smaller form !   Now winged he moved his white pin-
ions."

In these stories the greatness of his power is indicated.
This is less shown in that story which Ovid tells of him,
relating that on account of Daphne's beauty he wounded
Apollo, the conqueror of the Python, with a golden
arrow and Daphne with a leaden one, that he might love
her, but she might hate him.[31]

His beauty is thus described by Seneca, the writer of
tragedies, in the *Octavia* : [32]

"Human ignorance imagines that winged Love is a
cruel god, arms his sacred hands with weapons and with
bow, equips him with cruel torch and believes him the
son of Venus."

Servius, moreover, says that in age he is a boy and Franciscus de Barbarino, a man not to be disregarded, in cer-

[29] III. 60.
[30] ll. 294–301.
[31] *Met.* I. 452–77.

[32] ll. 557–60. *Arcusque sacros* of
the text cannot be right. I have
used *arcuque sacras* of the Loeb text.

tain of his popular poems binds his eyes with a bandage, gives him the feet of a griffin and surrounds him with a belt full of hearts.

Apuleius, moreover, when in the *Golden Ass* he describes the beauteous god sleeping, writes thus : [33] "When forsooth [she saw] the joyous hair of his golden head, perfumed with ambrosia, the curls, in fair disarray surrounding his white neck and rosy cheeks, some hanging in front, some behind, in dazzling splendor, the very light of the lamp trembled. Over the shoulders of the flying god dewy feathers like glistening flowers shone white, and although the wings were at rest, the soft, delicate tips trembled and stirred and ever played. The body, moreover, was smooth and luminous, one which Venus would not regret having borne."

Ausonius also tells a story about him recorded in a rather long poem, a story which he says was painted at Trèves in the triclinium of Zoilus.[34] Cupid by chance had flown through the myrtle-groves of Erebus and when the heroines who on account of him had suffered dire punishments and ignoble desires and deaths had recognized him, they formed a cohort and at once rushed against him. In vain he tried to exercise his strength. They captured him and against a lofty myrtle tree they fastened him on a cross and as he hung there hurled at him disgraceful charges. Among them, Ausonius says, Venus too came upbraiding him and reproaching him for Vulcan's chains and threatening cruel tortures. When some of his sins were disproved, others forgiven, they obtained pardon from Venus for him, and took him down from the cross. Then he himself flew away to the gods above. Many more stories too are told in addition, but

[33] *Met.* V. 22.　　　　　[34] Book VIII, *Cupido cruciatur.*

omitting these we must consider the significance of the words.

I think it is very possible that this Cupid was the son of Mars and Venus and famous for his beauty and wantonness. But about him they have not thought clearly in their inventions and, therefore, we must investigate in the opinions of more ancient writers what sort of person could have sprung from these gods. Now this one whom we call Cupid is a certain passion of the mind brought in from external causes, and introduced through the corporeal senses and approved for intrinsic qualities, when supercelestial bodies furnish aptitude for this. For the astrologers would have it, as my Venerabilis Andalo asserted, that when it happens on the birth of anyone that Mars is found in the house of Venus, in the bull forsooth or in the balance, the one who is then born will be a wanton sinner and will abuse all loves and be a man of evil in such matters. And on account of this by a certain philosopher whose name was Ali in the treatise on the fourfold division it was said that whenever on the birth of any one Venus participates together with Mars, she has to grant to the one born a disposition fit for wantonness and indulgences. This aptitude is developed so that, as soon as such a person sees some woman who makes an appeal to the external senses, at once the pleasure is reported to the inner perceptions and first imagination is stirred and then is transferred to thought. Moreover, from those sensations it is removed to that form of virtue which is nobler among the perceptions, that is, to a possible intellectual understanding. This is, however, the receptacle of sensible forms, as Aristotle testifies in the book *De Anima*.[35] There, moreover,

---

[35] Aristotle, *De Anima*, 424a 17, c. 12.

recognized and known, if it happens, through the will
of the one affected in which liberty of rejecting or re-
taining lies, that as if approved they are retained, then,
strengthened by memory, this passion for the thing approved, which now is called love or cupid, takes up its
abode in the desire of the senses, and there, driven on
by various causes, it sometimes is made so great and
powerful that it compels Jupiter to leave Olympus and
take the form of a bull.   Sometimes on the other hand,
not approved or strengthened, it slips back and is annihi-
lated by anger.   So then passion is not born from Mars
and Venus, but, in accordance with what was said above,
men fit for conceiving passion according to their bodies'
tendency are produced ; and if they do not exist, passion
is not generated.   So by a generous inheritance from Mars
and Venus as if from a somewhat more remote cause Cupid
is born.

Now Seneca, the writer of tragedies, in the *Octavia,* with
somewhat greater licence, but in fewer words, describes
his origin, saying : [36]

"A great power of the mind, a kindling flame of the
soul, Amor is born to youth, is fed on wantonness and
leisure amidst the happy blessings of fortune."

Surely in excuse of their own folly wretched mortals
oppressed by this passion have pretended that this pest
was a very powerful god, mortals whom Seneca, writer of
tragedies, describes in the *Hippolytus,* saying : [37]

"Lust doing homage to disgraceful servitude invented
that love was a god and, that it might be freer, conferred
on passion the title of an unreal deity."

But now we have come to the point that, having dis-
carded fictions, we should see what is hidden under them.
Men imagine that love is a boy that they may indicate

[36] ll. 561–63.   [37] ll. 195–97.

this is the time of life of those conceiving passion and their character. For there are many young men who sport like boys, and without self-control they are borne where the force of passion drives them, rather than where reason has ordered. Moreover, he is said to be winged that the passion of man may be marked as unstable. For trusting and longing, they easily fly from passion to passion. And more, it is imagined that he bears bow and arrows that the sudden captivity of foolish men may be symbolized, for they are conquered almost by a glance of the eye. They say these arrows are golden and leaden, that through the gold we may take delight since delight itself is bright and precious as gold. By the leaden arrows they mean hatred, for malevolence makes those on whom it lays hold as heavy and worthless as the metal.

Also a torch too is given to him which indicates the fires of the souls constantly burning, making men captives for their inconstancy. Moreover, they cover his eyes with a bandage that we may observe that lovers do not know where they are going, that there are no signboards for them, no differentiation of the roads, but they are led on by passion alone. Moreover, griffins' feet are given Amor that it may be made clear how tenacious passion is and that, when it has laid hold of the inactive and the idle, not easily is it loosened. The fact that he is fixed on a cross is, if we are wise, a warning which we heed indeed as often as recalling the soul to its powers by praiseworthy endeavor we overcome our softness and with clear eyes regain our vision, for we were being dragged along by our folly.

De voluptate filia Cupidinis. Cap. V.
About Joy daughter of Cupid

Joy, as Apuleius says, was the daughter of Cupid and Psyche. The story of her father was told above where the story of Psyche was fully related. The reason for this invention will be readily seen. For when it happens that we desire something and have obtained without doubt what we desired to possess, we are delighted. The ancients called this delight Joy.

Now having read Boccaccio's story of Cupid and Psyche and his interpretation of the myth, let us study his treatment. The telling of the story is characterized by the brevity which he commended, but the charm is not lost. The condensation of Apuleius' long story which was necessary for the *Genealogy* is effected by striking omissions.

These follow three lines. First, the characterization of Psyche's sisters, which Apuleius produced by their artful speeches to their ingenuous younger sister and their vituperative denunciations of their husbands to each other, is omitted. A few adjectives describe them ; their actions speak for themselves. Second, Psyche's tasks and the miraculous forms of aid given to her to complete them are not described. And third, the part of the Olympian gods in the story is greatly minimized. Venus' appeals to Ceres and Juno, Psyche's counter-appeals to Ceres and Juno are omitted. So are Venus' conversation with Jupiter, Cupid's conversation with Jupiter, the various dialogues with Mercury, and the Council of the gods. The wedding in heaven is only mentioned, not described brilliantly as in Apuleius. In other words the human side of the love-story of Love and the Soul is reduced to a simplicity of narration which prepares the way for the allegorical interpretation.

Before analyzing Boccaccio's moralization of the story, we must consider his own statements about the interpretation of myths. He refers, as Osgood has shown,[38] to three traditional systems : the fourfold mediaeval which includes the literal, the moral, the allegorical, and the anagogical ; Varro's triad of the mythical, the philosophical, and the popular ; and Augustine's variation of Varro's scheme with its euhemeristic emphasis.

Osgood summarizes clearly Boccaccio's "actual practice" which "derives from these three theories of interpretation" :

"A given legend, then, may be
(a) only the result of history glorified by the poets in honor of a great or ambitious man.   Such is its literal or historical sense, Varro's mythical 'theology,' or, more technically, euhemeristic myth. Or
(b) the story in a competent poet's hands may express allegorically the mysterious forces of nature, or of human life — the moral use, or 'allegorical' in the narrower sense, corresponding to the physical theology of Varro.   Or
(c) the story may conform to Christian truth, or adumbrate it in anagogical fashion.   The gods may really be but the angels and emissaries of God imperfectly understood without revelation, and even some myths gropingly shadow forth the Christian mysteries. Obviously the Platonic tradition lies behind this view."

Boccaccio though his "actual practice . . . derives from these three theories," uses no one system consistently.[39]   His aspiration may be seen in his definition of fiction as well as in his comments on it :

"Fiction is a form of discourse, which, under guise of invention illustrates or proves an idea ; and as its superficial aspect is removed, the meaning of the author is clear.   If, then, sense is revealed from under the veil of fiction, the composition of fiction is not idle nonsense."

"There are times, as in this book, when the theology of the Ancients will be seen to exhibit what is right and honorable, though in most such cases it should be considered rather physiology

[38] C. G. Osgood, *op. cit.*, pp. xviii–xix.

[39] H. Hauvette, *Étude Biographique et Littéraire*, Paris, 1914, pp. 426–27.

or ethology than theology, according as the myths embody the truth concerning physical nature or human.   But the old theology can sometimes be employed in the service of Catholic truth, if the fashioner of the myths should choose." [40]

These passages are significant for an understanding of Boccaccio's treatment of the hidden meaning in the Cupid and Psyche story.   In general he devotes himself to an allegorical interpretation, but he overlays allegory with language that is at times Platonic, at times Christian so that an anagogical interpretation is implicit in his words.

A review of the innumerable allegorical interpretations of the Cupid and Psyche story among the ancients and among Boccaccio's successors would have little value for the understanding of his words.   *Quot homines tot sententiae.*   From Fulgentius, who considered the King and Queen God and Matter, their three daughters Flesh, Free-Will and the Soul, and Venus Lust, to Hildebrand who believes that Apuleius' allegory is based on the mystic worship of Isis into which he had been initiated, every allegorical explanation takes color from the author and his times.[41]   Even though Friedländer, by emphasizing the folk-lore element in the story, laid the ghost of moralization, there have been and always will be certain mystics who will find the life of Everyman vaguely portrayed in the whole of Apuleius' *Metamorphoses,* and a true Greek romance of Love and the Soul in the old wife's tale told to Charite.   For such thinkers, who connect the very names Eros and Psyche with the vague Platonic sym-

[40] *De Gen. Deor.,* XIV. 9; C. G. Osgood, *op. cit.,* p. 48 ; *De Gen. Deor.,* XV. 8 ; C. G. Osgood, *op. cit.,* pp. 122–23.
[41] For allegorical interpretations of the Cupid and Psyche story see
    L. *Apuleii opera omnia,*
    Oudendorp-Hildebrand, Leipsic, 1842, Vol. I. pp. xxviii–xxxviii ;

L. Friedländer, *Roman Life and Manners Under the Early Empire,* translated by A. B. Gough, London, 1913.   Appendix XVII, especially pp. 99–101 ;
L. C. Purser, *The Story of Cupid and Psyche as related by Apuleius,* London, 1910, Excursus II, pp. 128–31.

bolism of certain poems in the Greek Anthology, Boccaccio will not seem to have gone far afield in his allegory
for his own times, so strongly influenced by neo-Platonic
thought.

For what has he done? Psyche is the Soul, child of
Apollo, the sun, "the true light of the world," and of
Endelichia, the perfect age. Her two sisters are functions of the soul, the nutritive and the quickening. Eros
is noble love or god himself. Psyche must accept her
husband by faith, not prove him by sight, for mortals may
not know the Omnipotent. Her sisters tempt her to sub-
stitute sensation for faith, and make her long to behold
her divine spouse though no one ever sees god. By following their advice she injures her relationship by losing
the power of contemplation. And she is separated from
god until, purified by toils and suffering, she is freed from
pride and disobedience, finds again the blessing of contemplation in god, and is made one with him forever.
What an inseparable web of Platonism and Christianity
is here firmly woven!

In another part of the *Genealogy,* Boccaccio discusses
Cupid's parentage, appearance, and functions.[42] His
method here is to quote a long line of ancient descriptions
of Cupid : Cicero, Ovid, Seneca, the writer of tragedies,
Servius, Apuleius, Ausonius, and a writer of his own
time, Francisco de Barbarino. From Apuleius he quotes
only the beautiful description of the sleeping god as
Psyche saw him !

In the interpretation of the traditional picture of the
god, Boccaccio turns to astrology for an explanation of
his wantonness through the conjunction of Mars and
Venus at his birth. Euhemerism appears in Boccaccio's
brief comment that *foolish* persons would make him a god

---

[42] *De Gen. Deor.* IX. 4.

of great power : "Surely in excuse of their own folly wretched mortals oppressed by this passion have pretended that this pest was a god." Really he is "a certain passion of the mind brought in from external causes and introduced through the corporeal senses."

So too his characteristics are figments of men's imagination. Cupid is a boy because passion is strongest in youth. He is winged because young love is unstable. His torch is a symbol of the fires of the soul. His eyes are bandaged because lovers cannot see where they are going. He is sometimes given griffins' feet because passion is tenacious. Once he was crucified as "a warning" to us to recall "the soul to its powers by praiseworthy endeavor" . . . "overcome our softness and with clear eyes regain our vision, for we were being dragged along by our folly." Boccaccio's interpretation here illustrates his use of astrology, euhemerism, and moral allegory.

This whole study of Boccaccio's varied uses of Apuleius demonstrates his *simpatia* with the Latin author. Boccaccio's several references to Apuleius' philosophical works betray the interest of the neo-Platonist in the *nobilis Platonicus.* The complete copy of Apuleius' works written from alpha to omega in Boccaccio's own hand shows the devotion of the book-lover who once wrote to Zanobi da Strada :

"I feel more joy over my few little books than kings feel over their great diadems" ;

"Plus cum aliquibus meis libellis parvulis voluptatis sentio, quam cum magno diademate sentiant reges." [43]

Finally, Boccaccio's brilliant use of two of Apuleius' Milesian tales in the *Decameron* and his charming retelling of Apuleius' story of Cupid and Psyche in Latin in minia-

[43] F. Corazzini, *Le lettere edite e inedite di Messer Giovanni Boccaccio,* Firenze, 1877, p. 36.

ture form show that the closest bond which held these kindred souls was their common art of narration. Both Apuleius and Boccaccio were led by the spirit of their times to mystic interpretation of the meaning of that fair story.[44] But beyond implicit or described allegory the tale itself has for each a self-sufficient justification as a form of art. Boccaccio, "poet, critic, scholar," owes his fame as did Apuleius, sophist, philosopher, and priest, to his peerless art of story-telling.

[44] For Apuleius see E. H. Haight, "Apuleius' Art of Story-Telling" in *Essays on Ancient Fiction*, New York, 1936, pp. 151–94.

VI

APOLLONIUS OF TYRE *AND SHAKESPEARE'S* PERICLES, PRINCE OF TYRE

Apollonius of Tyre was one of the most popular of ancient romances. This is proved by the persistence and the stability of its use.[1] From the first ancient allusion to it in the Sixth Century down to Elizabethan times it was translated into many languages, transformed into a novel, adapted to various poetic forms and finally gained its greatest fame through Shakespeare's *Pericles, Prince of Tyre*. Gower in the prologue to *Pericles* spoke the truth about the story :

> "It hath been sung at festivals,
> On ember-eves and holy-ales ;
> And lords and ladies in their lives
> Have read it for restoratives ;
> The purchase is to make men glorious ;
> Et bonum quo antiquius, eo melius."

That Latin line which "ancient Gower" inserted was appropriate, for the novel is written in the Latin language. Some indeed have thought that was its original medium, but scholars now generally agree that it is a Latin adaptation of a Greek original as was Apuleius' *Metamorphoses*. This has been concluded partly from its resemblance to the Greek Romances in general and

[1] Albert H. Smyth, *Shakespeare's Pericles and Apollonius of Tyre*, Philadelphia, 1898, p. 23.

to Xenophon of Ephesus in particular, also from the very fabric of the plot and the language. For interwoven with a typical Greek plot and conventional Greek themes are the old pagan mythology, a Christian diction taken from the Latin Vulgate and the use of the riddles of Symphosius, composed probably in the Fourth or Fifth Century.

The Greek original of *Apollonius of Tyre* from its language and style as well as from its many resemblances to the work of Xenophon of Ephesus belongs to the older type of the Greek love romances. That is, it would stand last in the group which, according to the new discoveries and the new dating, begins with the Ninus Romance (First Century B.C.), includes Chariton (before A.D. 150) and Xenophon of Ephesus (of about the close of the Second Century). The Greek original of *Apollonius of Tyre* may well have been written shortly after Xenophon's *Ephesiaca.*

The author of the Latin novel as well as the author of the Greek is unknown although at the end he seems nominally to identify himself with his hero. He wrote probably in the Fifth or Sixth Century.[2] The reasons for the dating are these. The romance was written before Venantius Fortunatus, bishop of Poitiers (566–68) in whose sacred lyrics is the earliest reference to Apollonius. It was composed in the period between Caracalla and Constantine because, as Smyth says:

"In chapter 34, forty aurii are considered more than a half libra auri, yet not a whole one ; that is, one pound of gold is coined into fifty pieces, which coincides with the practice of the time after Caracalla. After Constantine it became necessary to compute by solidi." [3]

[2] Erwin Rohde, *Der griechische Roman und seine Vorläufer,* Leipsic, 1914, pp. 435–53 ; Anhang von W. Schmid, p. 610 ; A. H. Smyth, *op. cit.,* pp. 17–23.

[3] A. H. Smyth, *op. cit.,* p. 22.

The translation was made after Symphosius, whose riddles, which are used in it, were composed probably in the Fourth or Fifth Century. The original Latin text of *Apollonius of Tyre* was therefore probably written in the Fifth Century, possibly in the Sixth.

The Latin romance is simple and short. It is written in a clear, simple style with short sentences. In these general characteristics as well as in many details it resembles Xenophon of Ephesus. In spite, however, of its brevity and simplicity it has many characters, and these it is desirable to list before proceeding to the narrative.

Antiochus, King of Antioch
His daughter
Her nurse
Thaliarchus, his steward
Apollonius, prince of Tyre
Hellenicus, of Tyre, an aged plebeian
Stranguillio, a citizen of Tharsus
Dionysias, his wife
Philomusia, his daughter
An old fisherman near Pentapolis
Archistrates, King of Pentapolis
Lucina,[4] his daughter
Three noble suitors of Lucina, one named *Ardalion*
The pilot of a ship from Antioch
Lycoris, the nurse of Lucina and Tharsia
Tharsia, daughter of Apollonius and Lucina
Chaeremon,[5] a doctor
A young medical student of Chaeremon

[4] The daughter of King Archistrates is not named in mss. A and P. But in cc. 29 and 49 the name *Lucina* was interpolated from a misunderstanding of the phrase in c. 25 "nono mense cogente Lucina enixa est puella." Since it is convenient to have some name for the princess I have adopted this Lucina.

[5] This name is found in ms. B.

Theophilus, the steward of Stranguillio and Dionysias
Pirates
Leoninus,[5] a procurer
The steward of the procurer
Athenagoras, a noble of Mytilene
Other young nobles of Mytilene
Girls in the brothel
The son of Apollonius and Lucina

Now follows the story.[6]
In the city of Antioch there was a certain King called
Antiochus, from whom the city itself received its name.
He had one daughter, a most beautiful girl. When she
was old enough to be married, she had many suitors, who
offered large dowries. When her father was trying to
decide to which one he should give his daughter, he fell
madly in love with her himself and finally one morning
at dawn raped her. Her nurse found her in her bedroom,
dissolved in tears and horror, meditating death. The
nurse soothed her and to prevent her suicide urged her to
accept her father's will.

Her impious sire, to keep her for himself, set a riddle
for all suitors to solve : anyone who tried and failed was
decapitated and his head was hung over the door of the
palace. One rich young man, Apollonius of Tyre, nothing daunted by the tales of Antiochus' cruelty came to
Antioch and entered the contest. The riddle ran :
"I am borne along by crime. I devour my mother's
flesh. I seek my brother, the husband of my mother, the
son of my wife. I do not find him." [7]
Apollonius by the help of god solved the riddle and

---

[5] This name is found in ms. B.
[6] My narrative is based on Alexander Riese's text, *Historia Apollonii*

Regis Tyri, Leipsic, 1893, constructed
from mss. A and P.
[7] Compare Oedipus' riddle in Seneca, *Phoenissae,* 131-39.

showed the King that he knew it referred to the incest between himself and his daughter. Antiochus declared he was wrong, but gave him thirty days for further study. The youth in horror at once departed on a ship to Tyre. Antiochus despatched after him his trusted servant Thaliarchus with orders to kill the Tyrian and a promise of his freedom as a reward for the murder. Meanwhile Apollonius reached home and, by consulting all the books of the philosophers and the Chaldeans in his library, made sure that his solution of the riddle was correct. Then knowing that his life was in danger he had a ship loaded with grain, and taking also much gold, silver, and clothing he set sail in the night with a few faithful slaves.

The next day when the citizens came to make their morning call they did not find him. The whole city went into mourning over his disappearance : the barbers had no business ; the shows were stopped ; the baths were closed. In this situation Thaliarchus arrived. Learning of the strange disappearance of Apollonius, he took the good news back to King Antiochus. That King offered large rewards for the capture of Apollonius, alive or dead.

Apollonius was informed of this when he landed at Tharsus by a fellow-citizen named Hellenicus who also had just arrived. Apollonius at first greeted him haughtily because Hellenicus was a plebeian, and then tried to reward him for his information with a gift of one hundred talents of gold, the King's price on his head. But the plebeian rebuked him saying : "Far be it from me, Sir, to take a reward for such a deed. Between good men friendship is not won by a reward."

As he walked on, Apollonius met another man, one whom he knew, named Stranguillio. He told him how Antiochus had proscribed him and begged to be con-

cealed in his city, but Stranguillio told him that Tharsus
was too poor to give him sanctuary : lack of grain had
brought the inhabitants to the verge of starvation. Joy-
fully then Apollonius offered to relieve the famine with
grain from his ship in exchange for refuge. The delighted citizens received him and set up in their forum
a bronze statue of their benefactor.

After a short time, on the advice of Stranguillio and his
wife, Dionysias, Apollonius again set sail for Pentapolis,
to take refuge there. But a terrible storm broke up his
ship and all on it except Apollonius perished. He was
washed ashore on a plank. There he met a poor old fisherman, wrapped in a sordid cloak, and begged him to give
aid to a shipwrecked prince. The fisherman in pity at
once led Apollonius into his hut, fed him, and then cut-
ting his cloak in two gave his guest half. He also advised him to go to the city to see if there he could not
find some patron, but if he did not, he was to return and
share a fisherman's luck and poverty. And the fisherman
begged Apollonius not to forget him if he was ever restored to his former rank and wealth.

When Apollonius entered the city, he found that the
gymnasium was just opened and the King of the city
Archistrates was entering it with a large retinue. Through
some god's help Apollonius was able to win the King's
favor by rapidity in playing ball with him and by dex-
terity in acting as his masseur after the game. The King,
finding that the man was a shipwrecked stranger, invited
him to dinner and gave him suitable garments. He bestowed on him also words of cheer when Apollonius sat
in sorrow in the midst of the conviviality.

Just then the King's young daughter entered, a beauty,
shining in gold ornaments. When she had kissed her
father and his friends, she inquired who the sad young

stranger was. The King urged her to make his acquaintance and try to cheer him. To her gentle sympathy
Apollonius told his story. Her father then urged her to
play her lyre to entertain the guests. All but Apollonius
heaped praises on her performance. He said she needed
instruction and to prove his point he begged to be allowed to demonstrate what lyre-playing should be. At
his playing all thought him not Apollonius but Apollo,
and the princess fell in love with him.

She persuaded her father to give considerable money,
twenty servants, and a large outfit of clothes to Apollonius
and then the King added a villa where he could live in
safety. Yet this was not enough to satisfy the princess'
ardor. In the middle of the night she rushed into her
father's bedroom and besought him to give her their guest
as a teacher. The next day this relationship was established. But alas ! this too was not enough for the young
princess. She became seriously ill of a malady which the
doctors could not diagnose.

Three noble young students of the town now offered
to the princess their hands and their fortunes. King
Archistrates, who divined all, sent Apollonius with their
three letters to his daughter's sick-room. The girl cried
out as he approached : "Why, my teacher, have you entered my bedroom in this singular way ?" Apollonius
answered : "My lady, you are just a little girl and you are
ill. Here, read the documents your father has sent you
and learn the names of your three suitors." When the
princess did not find the name she wished, she looked up
and said : "Professor Apollonius, aren't you sorry I am
going to get married ?"

"On the contrary, I congratulate you," he replied, "for
now that I have educated you, with god approving you

may marry your heart's desire." The princess said nothing, but gave him a sealed answer to carry to Archistrates. In it she said simply and directly : "Noble King and most excellent father, since through your kind indulgence you let me speak, I will. I want for my husband a poor shipwrecked stranger."

The King on receiving the letter put off the queries of the three suitors and handed the letter to Apollonius to read. He noticed with pleasure Apollonius' blushes and murmuring, "God's will be done," went home to his daughter. Her words made clearer even than her letter had her determination to wed her teacher. The King then told Apollonius all his child's desire and the Tyrian replied piously : "God's will be done if it be your will too !" The wedding was immediately celebrated with great splendor and joy, with music of cithara, lyre, organ and canticles. And their desire being fulfilled, the two felt a great love for each other, wonderful emotion, incomparable delight, unheard of felicity, which enfolded them in lasting tenderness.

Now the months passed and the young wife was going to have a child. One day as she and her husband were walking on the shore, they saw a fair ship which had put in there. It had come from Tyre and Apollonius learned from the pilot that the wicked King Antiochus and his daughter had been smitten by a thunderbolt from heaven and had perished ; also that his wealth and realm were being saved for prince Apollonius. Apollonius begged his wife to allow him to set forth to see his kingdom, but bursting into tears she said : "Dear husband, if you had been sent away somewhere on a long journey, certainly your duty would have been to hasten home for my accouchement. Now when you are here, do you propose to leave me behind ? Let us sail together. Wherever you shall be on sea or land, may life or death be the lot of both of us."

Then she went at once to her father, told him the good news of her husband's inheritance and asked him to allow her to sail with her husband. "And," she said, "that you may give your permission gladly, know you send away one, but you will welcome back two." The King, delighted with all this good news, ordered a ship to be made ready at once and stipulated only that an excellent midwife and nurse named Lycoris should accompany his daughter.

Unfavorable winds prolonged their voyage so that Lucina gave birth on the ship to a little girl, but she herself stopped breathing. While Apollonius was crazed with grief, the pilot of the ship came to him and told him that no ship which bore the dead could come to port, so he must at once bury his wife at sea. His slaves prepared a coffin lined with lead and in it Apollonius laid his wife. He placed twenty gold pieces by her head and gave her his last kiss. Then the coffin was consigned to the sea. Apollonius' only comfort was that he could take his little daughter home to her grandfather, King Archistrates.

On the third day thereafter the coffin was washed ashore at Ephesus near the estate of a certain doctor. As he was walking with his students, he discovered the box and had it brought at once to his villa. When it was opened there, he saw a beautiful young woman regally apparelled, twenty pieces of gold, and a letter begging whoever found the coffin to give this dear dead honorable burial. The doctor at once ordered that a funeral pyre be erected, but one of his students, a youth in appearance, but an old man in genius, closely studying the body, observed a spark of life. He told his teacher that he could resuscitate the lady, carried her to a bedroom and laid woolen cloths wet in hot oil upon her chest, until he started her circulation and she began to breathe deeply. At last she opened her eyes. Her first words were : "Doctor, I beg you not to touch me but as you should. For I am the wife of a King and a King's daughter." The student rushed in joy to his master and brought him in to approve his work. The doctor rewarded him with praise and ten pieces of gold. After a few days, under kind treatment, the young woman was able to tell her whole story. The doctor summoning his friends adopted her as his daughter. When she begged him to protect her, he secluded her among the priestesses of Diana.

Apollonius meanwhile, arriving at Tharsus, sought out Stranguillio and Dionysias. He entrusted to them the care of his baby, Tharsia, to be brought up with their own daughter and he left there too the nurse Lycoris. He gave them gold, silver, clothing, and swearing that he would never cut his beard, hair, or nails until his daughter should be married he sailed away as a merchant to distant lands in Egypt.

Tharsia was brought up as the child of Stranguillio and Dionysias. But when she was fourteen, her nurse Lycoris fell ill and, seeing death near, she told her charge all the story of her life : who her real parents were, how her mother died at sea. And the nurse gave her a farewell injunction : "After my death, if at any time your hosts, whom you call parents, do any injury to you, go up to the forum and you will find a statue of your father Apollonius. Embrace it and announce : 'I am the daughter of the man whose statue this is.' Then the citizens remembering your father's benefactions will protect you." Now the nurse died in Tharsia's arms. The young girl gave her honorable burial and after mourning for her a year went to school to acquire a liberal education. Every morning on her way home from school she stopped at her nurse's tomb to offer garlands there and pray to the manes of her parents.

On a certain holiday Dionysias took a walk with her daughter Philomusia and Tharsia. When she saw how all the people on the streets admired the beauty of Tharsia and her jewels and commented on the plain appearance of her own daughter, she was outraged. She resolved at once, since Apollonius had not been heard of for fourteen years, to put Tharsia out of the way and bestow her jewels on Philomusia. So she commissioned her steward to stab the girl on her way home from school and throw her body into the sea. When he protested in the name of the girl's innocence, she bribed him with promises of a large reward and his freedom.

The steward seized Tharsia in her nurse's tomb while she was calling upon the manes of her parents. He explained that her fortune and her jewels had driven her foster-parents to the deed and when she begged him to let her say her prayers before dying, he permitted it saying: "God knows not willingly do I commit this crime." While Tharsia was praying, pirates suddenly arrived, delivered the girl from her assailant and carried her off to sea. The steward on reporting to his mistress that the deed was done, was called by her a murderer and given no reward. Dionysias, however, told her horrified husband all that she had achieved and made him put on mourning with her to conceal the crime. She then announced to the people the sad death of their ward and the citizens, in honor of the benefactions of Tharsia's father, set up an inscription in bronze to her.

The pirates meanwhile arriving at Mytilene sold the girl at auction. A procurer outbid a noble named Athenagoras and put her in a brothel. The enamored Athenagoras was the first to approach her, but when Tharsia falling at his feet told him all her tragic story, he was overcome by pity, gave her a large fee and left her a virgin. In the same way her eloquence prevailed over each new visitor. The indignant bawd not content with his pure gains ordered his steward to corrupt the girl, but Tharsia persuaded him to let her earn money for her owner by giving concerts on her lyre each day in a public place. This plan proved a great success.

Now at last Apollonius returned to the city of Tharsus and was told by his false friends Stranguillio and Dionysias that his daughter had fallen ill and died. To prove their good faith they gave him all her jewels and showed him the monument and the inscription set up by the people of the city. Apollonius in despair returned to his ship, went into the darkness of the hold and lay there while the ship set off for Tyre. But unfavorable winds forced the crew to put in at Mytilene. It was the festival of Neptune. Apollonius gave ten gold pieces to each of the crew for a celebration, but forbade anyone to summon him on pain of having his leg broken. While the sailors were feasting on board, Athenagoras, who was walking on the shore, asked permission to inspect the ship. When he heard that the owner of the ship lay in the hold mourning for his wife and daughter and that no one of the crew dared approach him, he went down himself to try to rouse Apollonius. For Athenagoras on hearing the name Apollonius had a suspicion that this might be the father of the girl in the brothel who had said that was her father's name. When Apollonius only begged to be left alone, Athenagoras sent a lad to the procurer asking for the loan of Tharsia. After she was brought to the ship, Athenagoras commissioned her to bear comfort to the owner of the ship, who lay in the dark mourning his wife and child, and if she were successful in nursing him, he promised to buy her safety for thirty days from the bawd and give her ten gold pieces.

Tharsia went down into the hold and in a low voice said : "Greetings, whoever you are, be happy. I who come to bring you comfort am a pure maid, who in spite of shipwreck preserve my chastity." Then she sang him a little song, putting her own sad story into verse and begging him to lift his eyes to heaven for comfort. At the song Apollonius raised his head, looked at the girl and began to talk. He thanked her for her words of solace, but giving her two hundred gold pieces sent her away. Athenagoras promised her four hundred if she would go back and beg Apollonius to let her talk with him in the dark, since she came, not to make money, but to cure him.

This new appeal broke down Apollonius' resistance and he let her stay awhile. Tharsia to divert him proposed to him various riddles (ten in all) each of which Apollonius promptly solved. Then again he bade Tharsia leave him to the memory of his dead, and when she tried to draw him to the light, he struck her so that she fell down and blood gushed from her nostrils. Sitting there she bemoaned this new cruelty of fortune and once again related all her story. Apollonius hearing it to the end threw his arms about her and cried : "You are my daughter Tharsia. You are my only hope. You are the light of my eyes. Now may this city perish."

Athenagoras, who heard these words, rushing back to the city warned the people to save themselves by punishing the procurer. After Apollonius and Tharsia came to the forum, the citizens ordered that the bawd should be burned to death. But Tharsia spared the life of the steward because through his mercy she had been saved and she freed all the girls in the brothel. Apollonius made an eloquent speech of thanks to the people because his daughter had been kept safe for him and gave them a large sum of money to rebuild their fortifications. The citizens honored Apollonius and Tharsia by a group of statuary and an inscription. In a few days Apollonius let Athenagoras marry his daughter and then they all sailed away to Tyre.

Now in his dreams an angelic figure appeared to Apollonius bidding him direct his course to Ephesus and there in the temple of Diana with his daughter and his son-in-law relate all his misfortunes. Apollonius obeyed these orders and arriving at the temple of Diana, before the statue of the goddess and in the presence of the oldest of the priestesses, told his story. At the end the priestess with a loud cry announced : "I am your wife, the daughter of King Archistrates," and fell into his arms. To complete the joy of their reunion Apollonius presented her with their daughter Tharsia. All Ephesus rejoiced at the happiness of their priestess and bade her godspeed when she sailed away with her husband, her daughter, and her son-in-law.

Next Apollonius went to the city of Tharsus and there in the forum he summoned Stranguillio and Dionysias and revealed to the people their crimes through the evidence of the steward, Theophilus. When the two were found guilty, the people took them outside the city and stoned them to death. Theophilus was given his freedom. Then Apollonius voyaged on to Pentapolis in Cyrene and showed to King Archistrates his daughter Tharsia and her husband. They lived happily with the old King a year. Then he died bequeathing half his kingdom to Apollonius, half to his daughter.

One day walking near the sea Apollonius saw the old

fisherman who had befriended him. He gave orders to have him brought to the palace and reminding the old man of how he had shared his cloak with a shipwrecked stranger, he gave him money, servants, clothing and made him his comrade for life. ' The plebeian Hellenicus too, who had aided him when King Antiochus was pursuing him, he rewarded and made his companion. Now his wife bore him a son whom he made king in the place of his grandfather Archistrates. Apollonius lived with his wife seventy-four years in peace and happiness, ruling over Antioch and Tyre. Then after a happy old age they died.

On perusing this narrative, three elements strike the reader at once : the familiarity of the characters and the plot, certain definitely new features, and the strange mixture of pagan and Christian elements in the religious tone. The main features of the story, as in all the Greek Romances, are love, adventure, and religion, but these interests receive new directions or modifications. In the love romance there is not one story but two : the main plot involving Apollonius and the daughter of Archistrates and a sub-plot, the strange story of Athenagoras and Tharsia, the daughter of the first lovers. In addition to these two plots there is the introductory story of King Antiochus and his daughter.

It is in accordance with the tradition of the Greek Romances that an historical character is introduced at the beginning of the narrative to give a semblance of reality to the story. Antiochus the Great (222–187 B.C.) was a powerful eastern king, but there is no historical tradition of his committing incest or of his being killed by a thunderbolt. Bellinger suggests that this slander on his memory

"originated in the fact that in 196–5 B.C. he married his son Antiochus to his daughter Laodice. This marrying of full brothers and sisters was common enough among the Persian kings, but this is the first instance of the practice among the Greek monarchs of Asia Minor, and it may well have created a scandal." [8]

Since this prologue about Antiochus and his daughter is loosely attached and not properly integrated in the plot, Rohde suggested that the story of Antiochus was not in the original Greek romance. He thought that perhaps the Latin translator introduced this episode to take the place of the pagan oracle in Xenophon of Ephesus. Something was needed to motivate the travels of the prince of Tyre and since the Latin author was a Christian, he did not wish to use a pagan oracle.[9]

To me, however, the story of the wicked king Antiochus seems just the sort of prelude that a Greek sophist would have conceived for his double love-story in which the relation of father and daughter, Apollonius and Tharsia, played so striking a part. Nothing was dearer to the rhetorician's art than the principle of contrast, of antithesis. The story of the incestuous relation between Antiochus and his daughter, her corrupt nurse, the king's sadistic cruelty towards her other suitors, is a brilliant companion piece to the beautiful affection between Apollonius and Tharsia, the devotion of her nurse, her triumphal maintenance of her chastity. Shakespeare himself seems to point out this intentional contrast when he makes Pericles say to Marina in the recognition scene:

"Oh come hither,
Thou that begett'st him that did thee beget,"

lines surely reminiscent of Antiochus' riddle.

The contrast between the stories of Antiochus and his daughter and of Apollonius (Pericles) and his daughter is

[8] Alfred R. Bellinger, *Pericles, Prince of Tyre*, The Yale Shakespeare, New Haven, 1925, p. 95.

[9] E. Rohde, *op. cit.*, pp. 445-49; A. H. Smyth, *op. cit.*, pp. 15-17.

well brought out in Gower's last chorus in Shakespeare's play:

> "In Antiochus and his daughter you have heard
> Of monstrous lust the due and just reward ;
> In Pericles, his queen and daughter, seen —
> Although assail'd with fortune fierce and keen —
> Virtue preserv'd from fell destruction's blast,
> Led on by heaven, and crown'd with joy at last."

The motivation of the hero's travels is left equally vague in both Xenophon and Apollonius. Why Habrocomes and Anthia think they must fulfill the oracle by travel is obscure. Why Apollonius, after Antiochus died and he had wished to hasten to see his new kingdom, went to Egypt for fourteen years is unexplained. His disappearance may have been involved in his vow not to cut hair, nails, or beard until his daughter married, but this is not made clear.

The element of adventure in *Apollonius of Tyre* is much simplified. The background is set in only a few cities: Antioch, Tyre, Tharsus, Pentapolis, Mytilene. Long travels are not described although Apollonius was a wanderer for fourteen years. Marvels in strange countries which figured so largely in other romances, Achilles Tatius for example, have dropped out. A storm at sea is the chief purple patch and this is written in terms of child-birth and burial of the dead, a new method of description. As we shall see when we study the technique of the narrative, local color painted in by conversation and action takes the place of *purpurei panni*.

No one pagan deity is a dominant savior in the plot as in the Greek Romances. In fact, there are only a few references to pagan gods and these are conventional. Neptune is addressed as the ruler of the sea and his festival is celebrated at Mytilene.[10] Apollo is referred to as the god of the lyre.[11] Lucina as goddess of child-birth is merely mentioned.[12] In the temple of Diana at Ephesus the heroine finds a refuge among the chaste priestesses.[13] Tharsia prays daily to the manes of her parents, and votives are offered to the manes.[14] Priapus, covered with gold and gems, is the very present deity of the brothel.[15]

It is true that Apollonius finds his lost wife in the temple of Diana at Ephesus as in Xenophon Habrocomes found Anthia at the temple of Isis in Rhodes.[16] But Apollonius is directed to go to the Temple of Ephesus by an angel who appeared to him in a dream.[17] And it is a Christian faith and diction which thus points the way to salvation and pervades the story. *Deo volente* is a common phrase, as is also "thanks be to god." [18] "God's will be done" is uttered piously even by Apollonius when he is offered a princess' hand by her father.[19] The wicked Antiochus and his daughter are killed by a thunderbolt of god.[20] An assassin, Theophilus, allows Tharsia to pray to god before he murders her and exclaims : "God knows I am not willingly committing this crime." [21] Athenagoras tries to cheer the mourning Apollonius by saying : "I hope in god that he will give you after this overwhelming sorrow greater happiness." [22] Tharsia ends the song she sings to the despondent Apollonius with four lines of Christian consolation.[23]

Moreover, throughout the story the virtue of *pietas* is emphasized and it includes not only reverence for the

[10] C. 12, 39.
[11] C. 16.
[12] C. 25.
[13] C. 27.
[14] C.C. 30–32.
[15] C. 33.
[16] C. 48.
[17] C. 48.
[18] Examples are C.C. 17, 20.
[19] C. 22.
[20] C. 24.
[21] C. 31.
[22] C. 40.
[23] C. 41.

gods and filial devotion, but pity for the unfortunate : for
the young woman about to be murdered, for the slave-
girls in the brothel, for a man shipwrecked and in need.
And the virtue of this compassion is made as beautiful in
a plebeian gentleman and in a poor fisherman as in prince
or noble. Of course "the quality of mercy" was known
to the ancients,[24] but here the emphasis on *pietas* adds to
the Christian coloring of the novel given by the diction of
the Vulgate.

Against these main themes of the novel the characters
are drawn in general types, but with considerable in-
dividualization. Human relationships are brought out
through striking contrast. Three fathers are depicted in
their relation to their daughters : Antiochus the ab-
normal, who committed incest with his ; Apollonius, the
careless, who for fourteen years left his child to be
brought up by friends who proved false ; Archistrates,
who educated his daughter in liberal arts, in social
graces, in human sympathy and in the generosity befitting
a princess. Two heroines claim our attention, like
mother, like daughter. There are lively pictures of the
young blades of the times : Apollonius out for adventure,
braving decapitation in his first wooing, the three merry
gentlemen who were suitors of Archistrates' daughter, the
young sports of Mytilene who frequented the brothel.
The usual false friends of the Greek Romances appear in
Stranguillio and Dionysias. The minor characters include an old fisherman, a plebeian, pirates, citizens, slaves,
a bawd, girls of a brothel.

Antiochus the Great, an historical character, is presented as a foil to the noble Apollonius and Archistrates,
and is described with a crescendo of horror. Utterly corrupt, he raped his own beautiful daughter and then had

[24] Grace H. Macurdy, *The Quality of Mercy*, New Haven, 1940.

the arrogance to challenge all her suitors with a riddle which proclaimed his crime through a slight disguise. The heads of those who did not guess the meaning were cut off and hung over his palace door. "His impiety caused his crime," said his weeping daughter to her nurse as she planned suicide. But the nurse, an opportunist modelled perhaps on Phaedra's nurse, urged compliance to her father's will. Apollonius, who knew the King would murder him for guessing the riddle, started on his travels to avoid the King's sadistic vengeance and left his punishment to god.

Apollonius, the hero, is a complicated and emotional character. His love of adventure led him to become a suitor for Antiochus' daughter in spite of the danger. He was well educated : had a library of philosophers and Chaldeans, was an accomplished musician, a talented actor of both serious and comic parts, and a fine athlete. His intelligence was so lively that he solved not only Antiochus' conundrum, but all the ten riddles which Tharsia proposed to him. He was very proud in his youth : did not wish to talk to a plebeian, was reluctant to appear to engage in trade. But experience and misfortune taught him better values, so that finally he made lifelong friends of both plebeian and fisherman. He was always generous and distributed gold when he had it like a fairy prince. He was very emotional, weeping at a banquet over his misfortunes, blushing over the news that a princess loved him, refusing to be comforted for the loss of his daughter, brutally striking Tharsia when she tried to make him end his mourning. His sense of justice demanded that the procurer and the false friends who betrayed his trust should be punished. But he is made very *simpatico* in all his adventurous life so that the reader joins in the general rejoicing at his reunion with wife and daughter and at his length of days in peace, prosperity and happiness.

Apollonius' development to a stable and good ruler may have come from modelling himself on his distinguished father-in-law, Archistrates, king of Pentapolis. Archistrates' democratic spirit is shown in the first scene in the gymnasium, when he allowed the young shipwrecked stranger to play ball with him, then invited him home to dinner. His devotion to his daughter and his wisdom in bringing her up are apparent. He was proud of her accomplishments and her grace. He urged her to find out Apollonius' history tactfully and then to aid him generously as a princess should. He was very clever in his management of her suitors and in abetting her love for Apollonius. He celebrated the wedding with joy. Later he gave consent when his daughter wished to go on a voyage with her husband. His happiness was complete when after long years of separation, his daughter, Apollonius, their daughter and her husband returned to him to enrich his old age. And on his death he expressed equal confidence in his children by bequeathing half his kingdom to his daughter, half to Apollonius.

Lucina was indeed a princess of whom a father could be proud. From her first appearance at the banquet in all her youthful beauty, gleaming with golden jewelry, she captivated all eyes. She was winning, eager, sympathetic. The story of Apollonius' shipwreck and losses caught her imagination so that her heart went out to the stranger, and she was ready to trust her feeling and give all to love. Apollonius' criticism of her playing on the lyre aroused no resentment, only a wish to learn from him his own skill. She was spontaneous in telling her father her desires : first to have Apollonius as a *maestro,* then as her fiancé. Though she had to do the proposing, she

won and kept her hero's love. She would not be separated from him even though he must travel when she was
about to have a child, but convinced both her husband
and her father that her lot was cast with Apollonius' and
they were to live or die together. When she was rescued
from the coffin in which she was buried alive at sea, her
first and last thoughts were for her honor. So she became a priestess of Diana until god restored to her her
husband and her daughter. Her life was rounded out by
a happy year with her father, by bearing a son to Apollonius, seeing her daughter made a queen and ruling with
her husband through a long, peaceful old age. Lucina
was every inch a queen.

Her daughter Tharsia was a smaller edition of herself.
Though born at sea and consigned by her father to the
care of his friends for fourteen years, she had an unevent-
ful girlhood with her nurse Lycoris, believing Stranguillio and Dionysias her parents and going to school with
their daughter. At fourteen her tranquillity was shattered by learning from her nurse her true story and receiving a warning from Lycoris before she died about
possible danger from her foster parents. After a year of
mourning she returned to school, stopping every morning at Lycoris' tomb to offer garlands to her memory and
to pray to the spirits of her own parents whom she believed dead. There at this pious task the murderer sent
by Dionysias caught her and would grant to her inno-
cent piety only time for her prayers. That respite saved
her life, but her adventures then began, for pirates kidnapped her and eventually sold her to a procurer. In
the brothel all the young girl's powers came out, for she
persuaded every noble who entered her bedroom to pity
her and respect her chastity. When the bawd in despair
handed her over to his head slave to be broken, she per-

suaded that steward too to leave to her her honor and let her earn money for his master by public performances of recitations and lyre-playing.

When Athenagoras employed her to cheer Apollonius and win him back to life, her exquisite little song, her skill in proposing riddles, her pitiful horror when she was struck all endeared her. Out of the dark hold of the ship she emerged again a princess after the great recognition scene with her father and now went on from one happiness to another, for Athenagoras who had befriended her became her husband and fate gave her back not only her father, but her mother. The citizens of both Mytilene and Tharsus did her honor. Her sense of justice let her see the *leno* and her foster-parents executed. Her generosity saved the steward of the brothel and all the girls in it, even too the steward of Dionysias who in pity had given her a respite that saved her. At the end, Tharsia was the typical beautiful, virtuous, and happy Greek heroine.

Of the two false friends of Apollonius the woman was the leader of the deed of crime. Dionysias, deteriorating through envy of Tharsia's beauty and jewels and through jealousy for her own daughter, was presented as a foil to the pure devotion of Lucina for her child. Her husband Stranguillio was horrified at her malignity, but too weak to denounce her.

Athenagoras, the young noble of Mytilene, was ironic and mordant in his wit about the brothel episodes, but he was moved by pity for Tharsia, helped support her without reward, appreciated her accomplishments, tried to comfort Apollonius in his misery and then employed Tharsia to heal him by the charms of music. He won Tharsia's hand by his sympathy for her and her father.

Among the minor characters the pirates and the procurer are conventional types. The slaves are individualized : Lycoris by devotion and shrewdness ; Theophilus by his mercy and piety, the *villicus* of the *leno* by his response to Tharsia's appeal and his aid to her. This recognition of noble qualities in humble persons is further illustrated by the poor fisherman who like Saint Martin shared his cloak with Apollonius; and by the dignified old plebeian, Hellenicus, who scorned gold as a reward for friendly service. A few lines make these minor characters unforgettable.

The episodes through which these characters move are the usual ones of the Greek Romances:

> "Flight, wandering, captures, rescues, roaring seas,
> Robbers and prisons, pirates, hunger's grip ; . . .
> Pitiful partings . . . wedding bells." [25]

And the technique of narration employs the same devices as do the Greek Romances : a dream, a letter, inscriptions, apparent death, slavery, trials, résumés of adventures. There is also a startling resemblance to one special Greek romance, *Habrocomes and Anthia* by Xenophon of Ephesus. Common to both Xenophon and Apollonius is the main theme, the lasting power of true love. Certain cities which are pivotal in the plot are the same in both novels : Ephesus, Tyre, and Tharsus. Characters which both use are, besides the beautiful heroes and heroines, a physician of Ephesus, pirates, slaves, a procurer, an old fisherman, high officials of different cities. Smyth has summarized the general resemblance in action :

"The bold outlines of the narrative are common to both the Ephesiaca and the Apollonius. The marriage of the principal figures of the romance is in both instances at the beginning and not at the end of the adventures. The stories are alike in the in-

---

[25] Stephen Gaselee in *Daphnis and Chloe* in *The Loeb Classical Library*, New York, 1924, pp. 410–11.

tended assassination of the heroine by a slave commissioned by a jealous mistress ; the compassion of the murderer ; the escape of the heroine ; her preservation of her purity in a brothel, and the final recognition of the lovers in a temple by means of the hero's repetition in a loud voice of his adventures. Apollonius is succoured by an old fisherman of Cyrene ; Habrocomes sojourns with a fisherman of Syracuse. . . The wife of Apollonius is regarded by mistake as Artemis herself, and the same mistake is made with regard to Antheia." Rohde "finds in the brevity and dryness of the narrative an indication of a significant correspondence of manner in the two narrators, for the usual romantic style of the period was overflowing with pathos and color." [26]

Smyth might have elaborated other common features : the use of letter, dream, apparent death, shipwreck, trial-scenes, banquets, descriptions of works of art, the emphasis on the piety of the main characters. And as Chariton influenced Xenophon,[27] so Apollonius apparently took one episode from Chariton, the brutal blow given by the hero to a young woman.

Smyth was uncertain whether Apollonius imitated Xenophon or vice versa.[28] Perhaps, indeed, since the Greek original of *Apollonius of Tyre* is lost, no critic can make positive assertions about the relative dates of it and the *Ephesiaca*. We are safe in saying that these two Greek romances, the original version of *Apollonius of Tyre* and the *Ephesiaca*, belong to the same general type and to approximately the same period.

The style of Apollonius is characterized by simplicity, clarity and brevity. Sentences are short. There is much incidental conversation all through the novel and this is spirited. Some conversations are full of wit, as in the exchange of banter between two suitors of Lucina or the rueful admissions of the young nobles outside the brothel. Other remarks reveal character as in the plebeian Hel-

[26] A. H. Smyth, *op. cit.*, p. 12.
[27] E. H. Haight, *Essays on the* *Greek Romances*, New York, 1943, pp. 57–58.
[28] A. H. Smyth, *op. cit.*, p. 13.

lenicus' proud reply to Apollonius. Relationships are
developed by talk : that of Archistrates and his daughter,
that of the princess and Apollonius, that of Apollonius
and Tharsia in the ship's hold. Some speeches are highly
colored by emotion especially in Tharsia's words in her
nurse's tomb, in the brothel, in the ship.

No descriptions are introduced for decoration, but local
color is painted in pictures of everyday life : trial scenes
with rhetorical speeches, a brothel, a wedding, exercises
in the gymnasium, banquets with their entertainment,
two bedroom scenes, two recognition scenes. Votive
works of art are described enough to explain their significance in the plot : Apollonius standing in a biga holding grain in his right hand, his left foot planted on a
measure of grain because he relieved the famine of
Tharsus ; [29] and at Mytilene Apollonius holding his
daughter in his right arm and trampling on the head of
the procurer.[30] A conventional feature of all the Greek
Romances, frequent résumés of adventures, is constantly
employed.

A new feature of the narrative art, used before in the
Menippean satire, is the introduction of poems. These
are all in hexameters and consist of a description of a
storm, Tharsia's song of comfort, and her ten riddles.
The lines about the storm are too fragmentary to reconstruct, but the others deserve a place here for their nov-
elty.

Tharsia's Song to Apollonius in the Hold of the Ship

"Though o'er foul ways lies my journey, yet I myself walk uncor-
rupted,
  Just as a rose mid the thorns is not torn by the touch of their
  needles.
  Pirates once carried me off, for they struck with their unsheathed
  daggers.

[29] C. 10.   [30] C. 47.

Next to a bawd was I bartered, but never have sullied my honor.
Weeping and grieving and tears for my lost and my loved are my fortune.
None would be nobler than I if my father but found his dear daughter.
Now put an end to your weeping and throw off the weight of your sorrows.
Lift up your eyes unto heaven ; your soul to the stars lift up bravely.
God will be here to assist you, creator and author of all things.
He will not suffer these tears to be shed and your grief go unsolaced." [31]

This song with its touching autobiography and its Christian appeal at the end is a moving lyric. The riddles which Tharsia next propounds to Apollonius to divert him are amusing illustrations of the guessing games of the ancients.[32] I give them with Apollonius' correct answers.

Tharsia's Riddles

1. "There is a house in the land which echoes with clarion voices.
   Echoes the house itself, but the guest therein always is silent.
   Both natheless keep on running ; the guest and the house run to-gether."
   The wave and the fish.

2. "I'm the sweet friend of the bank, who doth dwell near the depths of the river.
   I, when I'm colored with black, make a song that is sweet to the Muses.
   Message am I of the tongue, which is writ by the hand of the master."
   The river-reed.

3. "Swiftly I'm borne on my way, tall daughter of beautiful forest.
   Great is the crowd of companions who make up my personal escort.
   Many the ways I run over, but never a trace leave behind me."
   A ship.

[31] C. 41.
[32] CC. 42, 43 ; quoted from Symphosius. See A. Baehrens, *Poetae Latini Minores*, 1882, IV. nos. 12, 2, 13, 89, 61, 63, 59, 69, 77, 78 ; also Raymond T. Ohl, *The Enigmas of Symphosius*, Philadelphia, 1928.

4. "Through my whole house ever enters and yet without burn-
    ing, the fire.
    Flames rise on this side and that ; they surround all the house
    yet I burn not.
    Stripped is my house and there also is stripped any guest who
    may enter."

    A bath (*balneum*).

5. "Two are the blades which are joined in the one steel unto my
    service.
    Struggle I now with the wind and now must I fight with the
    deep sea,
    Waters attack in mid-ocean, and clutch at the roots of the
    land's edge."

    An anchor.

6. "I myself am not heavy, but heavy the weight of my water.
    All my viscera swell, expanding in opening caverns.
    Hidden the water lies buried, and never pours forth of its own
    will."

    A sponge.

7. "Not with fair locks am I crowned, nor am I bedizened with
    ringlets.
    All of my hair is within, is within to be gazed at by no one.
    Me men toss in their hands, by their hands I am tossed in the
    high air."

    A ball.

8. "No sure figure have I, yet to me no figure is foreign.
    Bright is the gleam from within, for it shines with a radiant
    brilliance.
    Nothing whatever it pictures except what itself has before
    seen."

    A mirror.

9. "Four and alike are the sisters who run with such smoothness
    together.
    Just as if vying they run, yet all in their labor united.
    Close though they run and in time, yet they never can touch
    one another."

    Wheels.

10. "We are the ones who ascend to the skies in seeking high
    heaven.

Harmony binds us together in one, never broken, firm order.
Mortals who aim at the heights, must by us make their way
  to the ether."
The steps of a ladder.

Smyth suggests that when Tharsia tries to cheer Apollonius by proposing these riddles to him, "there is a
reminiscence of a popular kind of Oriental *märchen* in
which the sad and the sick are cheered and healed, by jug-
glers, mountebanks and fools." [33]   But Ohl has pointed
out that "among the Greeks, in whose estimation mental
agility was a virtue, the vogue of the riddle was wide-
spread and persistent." [34]   From the time of the riddle
of the sphinx which Oedipus solved, prophecies and oracles, charms, incantations, and imprecations "often took
an enigmatical form."   "Riddles and conundrums were
favorite aids to after-dinner conversation" as Athenaeus'
Deipnosophists (X. 69–88) shows.   The Romans too delighted in these guessing-games at dinner-parties as Tri-
malchio demonstrates at his famous *cena*.[35]   The use of
both Antiochus' incest riddle and Tharsia's enigmas in
Apollonius reflects the popularity of this kind of expression among the ancients.

We have already seen the Latin novel's resemblances to
the Greek Romances in general and to Xenophon of
Ephesus in particular.   In characters, background and
episodes, in simplicity and brevity of style, Apollonius is
closely related to Xenophon.   But just as Xenophon's
style was colored by Chariton's and Chariton's by Homer
and Longus' by Theocritus, so Apollonius is largely influenced by Vergil in structure and diction.   The fragmentary hexameters in C. 11 which describe the storm are
vaguely reminiscent of *Aeneid* I. 81–156 and VIII. 675–

---

[33] A. H. Smyth, *op. cit.*, pp. 13–14.   [35] Petronius, *Satyricon,* 58.
[34] R. T. Ohl, *op. cit.*, pp. 9–13.

713 in proper names and vocabulary. Far more striking however is the subtle way in which the meeting of Apollonius and the daughter of Archistrates at the banquet is made to resemble the hospitality given by Dido to Aeneas and her sympathy with his story. Archistrates is paraphrasing Vergil when he says to his daughter :

"ueteres ei renouasti dolores." [36]

And the description of the emotion aroused in the young princess by Apollonius' story is a cento made up of lines from the description of Dido which begins *Aeneid* IV :

"Sed 'regina' sui 'iam dudum saucia cura'
Apolloni 'figit in pectore uultus uerbaque,'
cantusque memor 'credit genus esse deorum.'
Nec somnum oculis 'nec membris dat cura quietem.' " [37]

I have already in connection with the religious elements in the story referred to the Christian episodes and vocabulary. Riese in the Index of his 1893 edition marks with a cross all words which appear only in this story and in Christian books and they are many. Riese also points out in his Preface that in Apollonius there are certain popular expressions which forecast usages of the Romance languages, for example the ablative in the phrase *in matrimonio postulabant, populi = homines, habet annos* like the French *il y a des ans,* and *quid est hoc quod* like the French *qu'est-ce que.* Apollonius in addition to offering us Vergiliana and a Christian phraseology is of some importance for learning the popular idiom of his time.[38]

Shakespeare's Pericles, Prince of Tyre

Once when I was working on the *Ephesiaca* of Xenophon of Ephesus, I had wished to see its cinematic plot

[36] C. 16 ; *Aeneid,* II. 3.
[37] C. 18 ; *Aeneid,* IV. 1–12.
[38] A. Riese, *op. cit.,* pp. xvi–xix.

transferred to the modern screen by some master film producer. Now I find a romance descended from him through the Greek to the Latin turned into a play by none other than Shakespeare. So in spite of the complicated maze of criticism which has been built around *Pericles, Prince of Tyre,* criticism involving sources, authorship, composition, I wish to present a few reflections on why this Greek romance was so popular on the stage in Shakespeare's day. For, on reading and re-reading *Pericles* aloud, I have been deeply impressed by its dramatic use of the story.

First of all we must consider how *Apollonius of Tyre* reached Shakespeare as a source. Ben Jonson's disparaging reference to Shakespeare's "small Latin and less Greek" hardly represents his knowledge of the classics. For in the grammar school of Stratford he must have read at least some of the Latin authors included in the curriculum of such schools, and these, after a study of Lilly's Latin Grammar were Baptista Mantuanus' *Eclogues,* Ovid, Vergil, Plautus and Terence, Caesar, Cicero, Sallust, Horace, and Seneca. References, quotations, and imitations in his plays and poems show a good reading knowledge of Latin, however much he used available translations.[39] His historical plays are based on Sir Thomas North's translation of Plutarch's *Lives,* but *The Comedy of Errors* is closely modelled on Plautus' *Menaechmi.* Shakespeare's language seems to embody many phrases from Seneca's tragedies. And from Ovid Shakespeare took not only the themes of *Venus and Adonis* and *The Rape of Lucrece,* but many mythological stories and some philosophy. So far as we know the *Menaechmi* and the

---

[39] H. R. D. Anders, *Shakespeare's Books,* a Dissertation on Shakespeare's Reading and the immediate Sources of his Works, Berlin, 1904.

Lucretia story in Ovid's *Fasti* (II. 721–852) had not yet been translated into English.[40]

How much Greek Shakespeare had is more debatable. Ben Jonson's phrase certainly indicates that he had some. By 1570 Greek was taught in certain grammar schools and Walter Roche, the headmaster of the Stratford school when Shakespeare entered it, had been a Fellow of Corpus College, Oxford, and so must have been a Greek scholar. It seems possible that Shakespeare had studied some Greek. Certainly he must have become familiar with the Greek tragedies through the Latin translations of the Complete Works of Aeschylus, Sophocles, and Euripides that had appeared between 1543 and 1597 as well as with volumes of Latin translations of selected plays and selected *sententiae*. Shakespeare too may have seen at Gray's Inn in 1566 the production of George Gascoigne's tragedy *Jocasta* which was based on Euripides' *Phoenissae*.[41]

At the antipodes in regard to the influence of Greek tragedy on Shakespeare, stand Sir Sidney Lee and J. Churton Collins. Lee declared dogmatically : "Such coincidences as have been detected between expressions in Greek plays and in Shakespeare seem due to accident, and not to any study either at school or elsewhere, of the Athenian drama." [42] Collins in three long, learned articles sought to demonstrate that in Shakespeare's plays there are so many instances of phraseology, *sententiae*, metaphors, sentiments, and characters which resemble those of the Greek tragedies that it is highly probable that

[40] Sidney Lee, *A Life of William Shakespeare*, John Murray, London, 1922, pp. 15–22 ; R. D. French, *The Comedy of Errors*, New Haven, 1926, pp. 76–81 ; J. Churton Collins, "Had Shakespeare Read the Greek Trage-dies ?" in *The Fortnightly Review*, 1903 (79), pp. 627–28.

[41] J. Churton Collins, *op. cit.*, pp. 623–25.

[42] Sidney Lee, *op. cit.*, p. 17 ; see also H. R. D. Anders, *op. cit.*, pp. 40 and 273–74.

he was influenced by them through the Latin translations which were easily accessible to him.[43] Collins himself is his own most severe critic of the inconclusiveness of such circumstantial evidence as he presents, but it seems to me that an unprejudiced reader of his articles may concede that he has made a good case for the probability of Shakespeare's acquaintance with the Greek tragedies.

Scant attention has been paid to his use of material from the Greek Romances. Yet Shakespeare himself shows that he knew Heliodorus' *Aethiopica* by an allusion to an episode in it :

> "Why should I not, had I the heart to do it,
> Like to the Egyptian thief at point of death,
> Kill what I love ?" [44]

And indeed many translations of Heliodorus were made during the Renaissance : ten editions of Amyot's French translation in the second half of the Sixteenth Century, four editions of Thomas Underdowne's English rendering in 1569, 1587, 1606, 1622. The romance of Theagenes and Chariclea was also dramatized and produced on the English stage as early as 1572–3.[45] Moreover, *King Lear* gets Gloucester and his sons from Sir Philip Sidney's *Arcadia* which took the plot of the *Paphlagonica* (*Arc.* II. X, 143–146) from Heliodorus.[46] *The Winter's Tale* is deeply indebted through Robert Greene's *Pandosto* to Longus' *Daphnis and Chloe* and the plot of Heliodorus' *Aethiopica.*[47] In the plot of *Romeo and Juliet* the ap-

[43] J. Churton Collins, *op. cit.*, 1903 (79), pp. 618–37, 848–58 ; 1903 (80), pp. 115–31.

[44] *Twelfth Night*, V. i, 121–23. The quotations from Shakespeare are from *The Oxford Shakespeare, The Complete Works of William Shakespeare*, edited by W. J. Craig, London, 1928.

[45] *British Museum Shakespeare Exhibition*, 1923. Guide to the mss. &

printed books exhibited in celebration of the tercentenary of the first folio Shakespeare with eight plates. Source Books. XV. 43 Heliodorus ; H. R. D. Anders, *op. cit.*, pp. 43–44.

[46] S. L. Wolff, *The Greek Romances in Elizabethan Prose Fiction*, New York, 1912, pp. 312–13.

[47] S. L. Wolff, *ibid.*, pp. 445–55 *et passim.*

parent death and entombment go back to Xenophon of Ephesus.[48]   And the story of Claudio and Hero in *Much Ado about Nothing* is to be traced through Bishop Bandello's XXII novella to Chaereas and Callirhoe in Chariton.[49]   Just so too *Pericles, Prince of Tyre* is a close dramatization of *Apollonius of Tyre,* however far removed it is in lineage from the original Greek romance. Let us now trace its descent.

The family tree of Shakespeare's play may be sketched roughly in this form :

A pagan Greek romance written in the II–III Centuries A.D.
A Latin translation written probably in the V Century A.D.
Godfrey of Viterbo's verse chronicle, *Pantheon,* XII Century.
John Gower's poem, *Confessio Amantis,* 1390.
A Latin version in the *Gesta Romanorum,* XIII–XIV Centuries.
Lawrence Twine's novel, *The Patterne of painefull Adventures,* 1576.
William Shakespeare, *Pericles, Prince of Tyre,* acted 1608, published 1609.
George Wilkins' novel, *The Painful Adventures of Pericles, Prince of Tyre,* 1608.

Gower admits his debt to

"a Cronique in daies gon,
The which is cleped Pantheon"

and to "olde bokes." Twine's novel is virtually a translation of the version of *Apollonius of Tyre* in the *Gesta Romanorum.*   Shakespeare is indebted to both Gower and to Twine.   Wilkins' novel on its title-page claimed to be "The true History of the Play of *Pericles,*" but followed also Twine's novel.

A detailed study of the inter-relation of these sources would be unprofitable here.[50]   Since Shakespeare is so

---

[48] G. L. Kittredge, *Romeo and Juliet,* Boston, 1940, p. xi.
[49] H. R. D. Anders, *op. cit.,* p. 65.

[50] For bibliography of such work see A. H. Smyth, *op. cit.,* 47–77 ; A. R. Bellinger, *op. cit.,* Appendices, A and C.

close to Twine, it is interesting to note in general what
Twine's variations from the Latin *Historia* (that is the
version in the *Gesta Romanorum*) were and his innovations. Smyth has briefly suggested them.[51] Analyzed
they amount to these : *purpurei panni* of descriptions including the storm at sea, the wedding of Apollonius and
Lucina (the costumes and jewelry of the guests, the dinner with its music and entertainments), the beauty of
Lucina when she was discovered in the chest ; also elaborate descriptions of emotions : Apollonius' grief on leaving Tharsus, the joys of Lucina and Apollonius on reunion, the terror of Stranguillio and Dionysias when
confronted with the living Tharsia ; general reflections on
the nature of love ; added, formal speeches. At the end
too Twine made one amusing addition in rounding out
the story of the pirates : he had them seized, but all set
free by Apollonius because they had preserved Tharsia's
life and, more than that, he had them all knighted !

Such was the chief source of the playwright who wrote
Pericles, Prince of Tyre : a novel that followed very
closely the traditional old Latin versions of the story, with
additions of descriptions, of expansion of emotional passages, and of some general reflections. In *Pericles* these
accretions drop away. The main narrative is closely followed and a new richness of characterization appears.

Pericles is probably, as Mackail says, the first play
Shakespeare wrote in "the new movement" in the treatment of drama to what is conveniently called "romance."
In these later years belong, after *Pericles*, *Cymbeline*, *The
Winter's Tale* and *The Tempest*. "The romantic
drama," Mackail comments, "had originated in the
dramatization of the novel," and these plays "are alike
. . . in the way in which (as is the manner of romances)

---

[51] A. H. Smyth, *op. cit.*, p. 74.

they transport us from land to land, from courts to caves and cottages ; even, in *The Winter's Tale,* from one generation to another." [52]

Before we try to understand the qualities which made *Pericles, Prince of Tyre* such a success on the stage in Shakespeare's time, we must briefly mention the controversies which have raged about its authorship and composition. The unexplained fact that it was excluded from the First and Second Folios started the discussion of the authorship. Dryden (1684) dated it as an early play, but Pope believed it spurious. Malone (1780) accepted it as an early work, but Stevens (1790) believed in a double authorship. Theories about date, authorship, and construction continued to pair off in antitheses. Present opinion seems to agree that it is a late play, but holds it to be only in part the work of Shakespeare himself.

Under this general consensus of opinion, three questions arise to which only tentative answers can be given.[53] First, how much of the play is attributable to Shakespeare? One theory is that "Shakespeare is the sole author . . . but the play combines two periods of his life." [54] Another answer to this question is that Shakespeare wrote occasional passages of the first two acts and all of acts III, IV and V except the tetrameter choruses. A second question then arises : if Shakespeare did not write all the play, who wrote the rest ? George Wilkins is the preferred candidate here with Thomas Heywood running as a not very close second. Certain critics, who regard the brothel scenes as non-Shakespearean because of their coarseness, suggest as possible authors of these scenes Row-

[52] J. W. Mackail, *The Approach to Shakespeare,* Clarendon Press, Oxford, 1933, pp. 99–100.

[53] A. R. Bellinger, *op. cit.,* Appendix C., A. H. Smyth, *op. cit.,* pp. 64–69 ; Sidney Lee, *Shakespeare's Peri-* *cles,* being a reproduction in facsimile of the First Edition 1609 from the copy in the Malone collection in the Bodleian Library, Clarendon Press, Oxford, 1905, pp. 13–14.

[54] A. H. Smyth, *op. cit.,* p. 64.

ley, Dekker, and Chapman, but they can advance no proof for such attributions.

The third question is, if Shakespeare did not write the whole play, did his contribution precede or follow the work of the other author or authors ?   One theory is that Shakespeare revised some one else's play.   Another is that Shakespeare originally wrote "The Story of Marina," in the last three acts, and this material was expanded by some one else to a five act play.   I pose these questions simply to suggest the complexity of the problems surrounding the authorship and composition of what was probably Shakespeare's earliest experiment in the field of romance.   My comments on the play may explain why I incline (without proof) to the theory that Shakespeare wrote *Pericles, Prince of Tyre* at two periods of his life and never completed his revision.

On reading and re-reading the play as it stands in an unabridged text, I find that the most striking feature is its fidelity to the traditional story of the old Greek romance. Smyth has illustrated the persistence and the stability of the story by descriptions of versions appearing in many languages : German, Swedish, Danish, Dutch, Hungarian, Italian, Spanish, Provençal and French, Modern Greek and Russian.[55]   Shakespeare's play is as true to the traditional old plot as any of these.   Yet within this pattern he makes innovations in structure and character-drawing that show the master playwright's hand.   I shall speak of "Shakespeare's *Pericles*," proceeding on the assumption that the whole play was planned by him, and that it was written at two periods with a partial revision at the second writing.

For clarification of the story, the changes in names must be mentioned first.   Apollonius becomes Pericles, possi-

---

[55] A. H. Smyth, *op. cit.*, pp. 25–48.

bly because Sidney's hero in the *Arcadia* was named Pyro-
cles. Of other leading characters, Athenagoras becomes
Lysimachus. Archistrates is now Simonides, Hellenicus
is Helicanus. Stranguillio is Cleon and his wife Dionysias is Dionyza. The princess of Pentapolis is Thaisa and
her daughter is Marina. There are other minor changes.
Shakespeare uses Gower's forms of names wherever they
differ from Twine's. In three names he differs from the
usages of all the authorities : Pericles, his wife Thaisa,
Marina.[56]

The three most striking changes in the plot of the Latin
Historia are the addition of the Gower chorus : the introduction of dumb shows ; the omission of all the riddles
except the first and the addition of Thaisa's learned ex-
planations of the devices of the knights. As one of Shakespeare's sources was John Gower's *Confessio Amantis*, it
was a stroke of genius to introduce the fourteenth-century
English poet as Chorus. Gower speaks prologue and
epilogue, appears at the beginning of each act as well as
before Act IV, Scene 4 and Act V, Scene 2, and, as the
Chorus, carries the narrative of parts of the story not
enacted on the stage. There is such a chorus in *Henry V*,
in *The Winter's Tale* and in other Elizabethan plays.
These choruses are a direct inheritance from Greek tragedy through Seneca.[57] The differences in the Elizabethan use is notable, for as Bellinger comments :

"The ancient chorus was present on the stage throughout the
play, and its function was to supplement the action by moral ob-
servations, or ornament it by purely lyric passages ; it was not
used, as here, to supply information otherwise inaccessible to the
audience."

[56] A. H. Smyth, *op. cit.*, pp. 70–72 ;
Sidney Lee, *Shakespeare's Pericles*,
pp. 9–10.

[57] A. R. Bellinger, *op. cit.*, p. 93 ;
Clarence W. Mendell, *Our Seneca*,
New Haven, 1941, chap. VII, "The
Chorus."

Gower himself says of his function :

> "I do beseech you
> To learn of me, who stand i' the gaps to teach you
> The stages of our story."

The choruses in the first three acts use Gower's own meter, the iambic tetrameter, in rhyming couplets, but in Acts IV and V the meter shifts to the iambic pentameter. This difference in meter to certain critics involves different authorship.   It may as well involve lack of revision.

In the beginning of both Act II and Act III dumb shows interrupt the chorus to vivify by pantomime the action supplied by Gower's narration.   In each case a letter is presented, which brings in the first instance bad news, in the second good news.   Such dumb shows were used also in *Cymbeline* and in the mimic play in *Hamlet*.   Their pageantry apparently suited the Elizabethan taste.

Guessing games, however, seem to have gone out of fashion.   Twine in his novel retained only three of Tharsia's ten riddles.   Shakespeare uses only the incest riddle of King Antiochus.   To display his heroines' learning he does not have Marina propose riddles to Pericles but instead has her mother Thaisa explain at the banquet to her father Simonides the devices on the knights' shields, including their mottoes in Latin and Spanish.

Besides these three major changes, there are alterations in details partly for simplification, partly to contemporize the set.   Shakespeare makes Antiochus allow Pericles a respite of forty days to study the riddle while the Latin mentions thirty.   Shakespeare also simplifies Apollonius' vow about his period of mourning to

"Unscissar'd shall this hair of mine remain,"

although the Latin and Twine make Apollonius include untrimmed beard and unpared nails in his resolution.

Elizabethan color is given by having the suitors of Thaisa "joust and tourney for her love" and in adding to king Simonides' banquet "a soldier's dance." The brutal blow which in the Latin was given by the mourning Apollonius to Tharsia is modified in Shakespeare to some "violence," against which Marina protests and which Pericles acknowledges.[58]   Yet the brutal blow of a lover is part of the tradition of the Greek Romances, going back from Apollonius to Chariton.[59]

Some significant descriptions are added by Shakespeare. These are the terrible account of the famine in Tharsus, the tremendous picture of the storm at sea, in which the young mother was supposed to have died in child-birth, and the portraits of Thaisa in the chest when it is opened by Cerimon, and of Marina in the famous speech where Pericles compares her to her mother :

"My dearest wife was like this maid."

There is a difference also in the use of music in the set. A lyric quality in the story is emphasized in Gower's opening chorus :

"To sing a song that old was sung
From ashes ancient Gower is come.
. . .

If you, born in these latter times,
When wit's more ripe, accept my rimes,
And that to hear an old man sing
May to your wishes pleasure bring,
I life would wish, and that I might
Waste it for you like taper-light."

There are several instances where the lines demand incidental music.   Simonides at his banquet refers to "loud

---

[58] V. i, ll. 128–29. Smyth, *op. cit.*, p. 73 fails to see that Pericles acknowledges this "violence."

[59] E. H. Haight, *op. cit.*, pp. 17, 20.

music" for "a soldier's dance." The physician Cerimon
when he is seeking to revive Thaisa orders :

> "The rough and woeful music that we have,
> Cause it to sound, beseech you.
> The viol once more."

Pericles before Diana appears to him in a vision keeps
hearing

> "The music of the spheres . . .
> Most heavenly music." [60]

Music is considered an essential part of education, for
Pericles taught it to Thaisa and Marina was

> "by Cleon train'd
> In music, letters,"
> and   "to the lute
> She sung, and made the night-bird mute."

Two pieces of evidence of lack of revision in the play
are concerned with music. Simonides thanks Pericles
for his "sweet music" at his banquet, declaring :

> "Sir, you are music's master,"

but in Shakespeare Pericles has not performed at all at
the banquet and this reference goes back to the Latin story
where the stranger guest Apollonius taught the young
princess what true music was by playing on the lyre.

Later in the play when Marina is brought by Lysimachus to console by her music the melancholy Pericles,
the stage direction in the first edition says "The Song,"
but the song is not given. Yet her lyric is an essential part
of the old Latin versions.[61] Since Shakespeare has not in-

[60] On this Pythagorean and Platonic theory of "the harmony of the
spheres" and other references to it in
Shakespeare, see H. R. D. Anders,
op. cit., p. 241.

[61] Mackail apparently overlooked
this. See J. W. Mackail, *op. cit.*, p.
96 ; Sidney Lee, *Shakespeare's Pericles*, V. i, 80.

serted her song here, I am inclined to think that perhaps
he used Twine's beautiful rendering of the Latin hexameters. For here was an Elizabethan lyric made to his
hand. I quote it to show how much it would add to this
scene.

The Song,
translated by Lawrence Twine

"Among the harlots foule I walke,
    yet harlot none am I :
The Rose amongst the Thorns grows,
    and is not hurt thereby.
The thiefe that stole me, sure I thinke,
    is slaine before this time,
A bawd me bought, yet am I not
    defilde by fleshly crime.
Were nothing pleasanter to me,
    than parents mine to know :
I am the issue of a king,
    my blood from kings doth flow.
I hope that God will mend my state,
    and send a better day.
Leave off your teares, plucke up your heart,
    and banish care away.
Shew gladnesse in your countenance,
    cast up your cheerfull eyes :
That God remaines that once of nought
    created earth and skies.
He will not let in care and thought
    you still to live, and all for nought." [62]

Besides these innovations on Shakespeare's part, certain
characters undergo vital changes. Helicanus is no longer
the noble plebeian of the traditional story, but a noble
in rank as well as in name, to whom Pericles entrusts his
realm in his absence. Also the physician Cerimon is
made one of the most important characters, for his pupil
who restored Lucina to life in the ancient romance is
changed to a mere servant and all honor for "virtue and

[62] *Shakespeare's Library*, London, 1875, Part I, vol. IV, pp. 307–308.

cunning" is bestowed upon the great physician of Ephesus
to whom it is said

> "hundreds call themselves
> Your creatures, who by you have been restor'd ;
> And not your knowledge, your personal pain, but even
> Your purse, still open, hath built Lord Cerimon
> Such strong renown as time shall ne'er decay."

Additional characters are also added, particularly
Escanes, another lord in Pericles' service. There are
three fishermen instead of one on the coast where Pericles
is shipwrecked, a change which permits a fine prose scene
of racy, common talk. And there are also three bawds
instead of two to make the brothel scenes more venal and
more coarsely realistic.

In spite of these variations and changes in *Pericles,
Prince of Tyre* the play is fundamentally a classical play.
This style is given to it first by the chorus which descended
from Greek tragedy through Seneca's reshaping. And as
in Greek tragedy the particular myth used, which was
familiar to the audience, was preserved in its entirety in
the plot which changes inside its framework, so here the
traditional old Greek romance, retold in Latin, of *Apollonius of Tyre* is the essential, indestructible fabric of
Shakespeare's play. Hence inevitably certain striking
scenes which some modern critics would eliminate must
be kept : the story of Antiochus' incest, which exposes the
hero to the horrors of lust ; the brothel scenes which ex-
pose the heroine to attacks on her chastity. For these
scenes are vital elements in the original Greek sophist's
art of composition, making virtue fairer by startling antithesis. The purity of Marina shines white by contrast
with Antiochus' daughter and with the rotten creatures,
the little beggars of the brothel.

That Shakespeare was fully aware of the value of the

contrast between the relations of Antiochus and his daughter and Pericles and his daughter is suggested in a line rich in connotation. In the great recognition scene between Pericles and Marina, he cries to her :

> "O ! come hither,
> Thou that begett'st him that did thee beget."

In this spiritual symbolism of life restored there is definite reminiscence of Antiochus' incest riddle. Thus in the two pairs of father and daughter we have portrayal of an unholy and a holy Electra complex, in the language of the psychoanalysts, the well-known obverse of the Oedipus complex.[63]

Shakespeare is akin to Euripides in his handling of humble characters, for he brings out the hospitality of an old fisherman as Euripides brought out the generosity of Electra's peasant husband. And the great recognition scene at the end of Pericles' story is vaguely reminiscent of Alcestis' restoration to her husband after death and burial. Of that romantic tragedy, *Pericles, Prince of Tyre* seems to be a descendant as well as of Greek romance.[64] And like Euripides, Shakespeare made changes within the strict framework of his myth on the lines of an extension and a deepening of human interest and of a development of individual characters. Although *Pericles, Prince of Tyre* as it stands is a play that needed more revision, I believe that it was the genius of Shakespeare which

[63] Charles Baudouin, *Psychoanalysis and Aesthetics*, London, 1924, p. 236.

[64] "The Alcestis *motif* which appears here is more clearly introduced in *The Winter's Tale*," and "it is in regard to the story of the queen that Shakespeare differs most from Greene. . . . No English adaptation of the *Alcestis* is known to have existed before the date of *The Winter's Tale* (1610–11), but it is not impossible that Shakespeare read the play in a literal Latin version, such as Stephens' (1567). The influence of the *Alcestis* may be traced again in the character of Katharine in *Henry VIII*." From P. G. Thomas, *The Shakespeare Library : Greene's 'Pandosto' or 'Dorastus and Fawnia,'* New York, 1907, pp. xvi–xvii.

made the general plan for it, kept it true to classical, dramatic tradition and out of a Greek romance constructed the first of his romantic plays.

Critics might carp at its inadequacies. Ben Jonson dubbed it "a mouldy tale," composed of "scraps out of every dish," which suited the taste of "a loathsome age," in which

> "sweepings do as well
> As the best-ordered meal." [65]

Later Dryden excused its imperfections on the ground of its being an early work :

> "Shakespeare's own muse his *Pericles* first bore ;
> The Prince of Tyre was older than the Moor ;
> 'Tis miracle to see a first good play ;
> All hawthorns do not bloom on Christmas Day." [66]

But with the theater-going public the play was long a favorite.

Its popularity both on the stage and among readers is attested by ample evidence, Lee says :

"There were at least six editions issued within twenty-six years of its production. . . Numerous references to the piece in contemporary literature attest the warm welcome which the public extended to its early representations. . . On May 24, 1619 the piece was performed at Court on the occasion of a great entertainment in honour of the French ambassador, the Marquis de Trenouille. . . On June 10, 1631, the piece was revived before a crowded audience at the Globe Theatre 'upon the cessation of the plague.' At the Restoration *Pericles* renewed its popularity in the theatre." [67]

The theater-going pubic welcomed the play for its deep humanity and its true romance. Here are two royal heroines of peerless virtue and beauty, mother and daugh-

---

[65] Ben Jonson, *Ode to Himself.*
[66] Prologue to Davenant's *Circe*, 1675.

[67] Sidney Lee, *Shakespeare's Pericles,* Clarendon Press, Oxford, 1905, pp. 17–20.

ter, and no such pair ever deserved more completely Horace's line,

O matre pulchra filia pulchrior.

Pericles is the truly romantic hero starting off for adventure in quest of a golden girl and ready to

"Think death no hazard in this enterprise."

Since his heart is pure, he scorns the beauty of his first "fair glass of light," Antiochus' daughter, when he knows the "glorious casket stor'd with ill." Bereft of all worldly possessions by shipwreck he finds his true love in adversity and then in adversity loses her. His tenderness for his wife in child-birth and for the little daughter born at sea prepares us for his black melancholy when he believes them both lost. The depth of his feeling creates the intensity of the recognition scenes. What other play ever put on two recognition scenes without anticlimax? Equally moving are the one between father and daughter and the one between husband and wife with daughter added to complete the bliss of reunion. Diana and god were indeed beneficent to bring such happiness out of disasters. Pagan and Christian deities unite their blessings as in the Latin version of the traditional old story.

The unassailable purity of hero and of heroines is set off by the story of incest and by the scenes in the brothel. The playwright's audacity made the most of these contrasts sparing his audience nothing of the ugliness of lust. And with the trick of the old Greek rhetorician's antithesis Shakespeare in his two prose scenes of common life contrasted the homely wit of his three "honest fishermen" with the heartless, racy vulgarity of Pandar, Bawd and Boult in their unhallow'd business. These startling contrasts in the play, these bold presentations of common and unsavoury scenes, these excitements of adventure, the lyric passages of rare beauty, the happy ending of true love, and the touching loveliness of young Marina are the great features which made the play a tremendous success upon the Elizabethan stage. And the Greek story was easily adapted to the English mind by letting ancient Gower relate much of it as "our play."

Would it be possible to revive *Pericles, Prince of Tyre* on the modern stage ? Margaret Webster, foremost producer of Shakespeare in this country, thinks not. Her reasons are interesting. Although she sees collaboration in the composition of the play and some bad writing, she would redeem for Shakespeare even parts of the first two acts, and certainly the brothel scenes, since, though "they sound a harsh discord in the lyric of the play . . . it is a Shakespearean dissonance. . . Marina, decked, like Perdita, with flowers of springtime delicacy, moves through them with a white ardor." Miss Webster, indeed, ranks Marina with Perdita and Miranda among Shakespeare's heroines of romance. But the artificialities of the plot, the expense of an adequate production, and the incredulity of the modern audience over miracles must deter, she believes, an appreciative producer from risking *Pericles*. Let Miss Webster speak for herself :

"The story has meandered a long way ; it has been, of itself, consciously artificial ; and, worst theatre fault of all, its diverse episodes, separated widely in space and time, are bridged by no such dramatic scheme as Shakespeare has been at pains to devise for his great plays. They are arbitrarily linked by a narrator, who describes the intervening events in deliberately archaic octosyllable couplets. If the play is done at all, it must have the quality of an idyll of the golden age and be set luminously and richly. It was a hit, apparently, throughout its early career and retains at least some of the essential elements which made it so. But we should have to cut and tighten, drench the scenes with music, and play it like a decorative tapestry for the eye. It is a play for a relaxed and leisured audience, not too demanding, ready to accept make-believe.   Until such time as we evolve a company and an audience who take pleasure in Shakespeare for Shakespeare's sake, we are unlikely to see much of *Pericles.*" [68]

Perhaps some Experimental Theater is the one to dare a revival of this play so popular in Shakespeare's time. Certainly a production of this classical romance would be illuminating for the appreciation of Shakespeare's last plays, *Cymbeline, The Winter's Tale, The Tempest.* And the full values of *Pericles, Prince of Tyre* can never be tested until it is seen on the stage.   Personally, I believe a production with great actors, simple scenery, and haunting music would project the deep humanity of the play across the foot-lights, for I think Shakespeare's genius flares high in *Pericles,* as even George Lillo, the playwright who was the first to question Shakespeare's authorship of the whole play, admits:

> "We dare not charge the whole unequal play
> Of *Pericles* on him ; yet let us say,
> As gold though mix'd with baser matter shines,
> So do his bright inimitable lines
> Throughout those rude wild scenes distinguish'd stand,
> And shew he touch'd them with no sparing hand." [69]

[68] Margaret Webster, *Shakespeare without Tears,* New York, 1942, pp. 38, 41, 96–97, 272–75.

[69] Sidney Lee, *op. cit.,* p. 20.

APPENDIX I

Outline of Alexander's life based partly on W. W. Tarn, *The Cambridge Ancient History*, vol. VI and G. Radet, *Alexandre le Grand*.

Facts	*Tendencies and Ideologies*
356 B.C. Born at Pella. childhood and youth.	Influences : 1. of mythology : descent from Zeus ; devotion to *Iliad*. 2. of Aristotle : teaching that Greeks were superior to barbarians ; the city-state. 3. of Philip : the pan-Hellenic ideal; the military ideal : 4. of the east : conversation with the ambassadors from Darius.
336 Murder of Philip and accession of Alexander. Alexander elected general of the Greeks by the League of Corinth.	The Pan-Hellenic ideal ; the unification of Greece.

335 Destruction of Thebes.	Military conquest.
334 Campaign in Asia Minor :	
Battle of Granicus.	Gave up old military tactics : led cavalry in person as an epic hero, the new Achilles.
Visit to Troy.	
Democracies set up in Ionia.	Ideal : liberation and renaissance for the Greeks in Ionia.
333 The Battle of Issus.	
Foundation of Alexandria.	Aspiration for eternal fame in perpetuation of his name.
Visit to shrine of Ammon.	Beginning of acceptance of oriental ideas : the divinity of the king ; universal conquest.
331 The Battle of Gaugamela.	
Occupation of Babylon, Susa, Persepolis.	Beginnings of development of a combination of

Beginnings of development of a combination of
1. oriental mysticism, half religious, half imperial ;
2. realistic military preparation for world domination.

Steps in orientalization of Alexander's ideas :
1. rejected Darius' three offers of terms of peace, looking to world domination ;

2. after visit to Cyrus' tomb at Pasargades Alexander began to think of himself as the new *Cyrus,* the ideal Oriental sovereign who united the nations in a fraternal peace.

330 First Dionysiac revel at Persepolis : the burning of the palace.

The death of Darius : terrible punishment of Bessus.

Oriental barbarism in his execution.

The Macedonians in the army struggle against Orientalization :

their conspiracy ;

the trial and execution of Philotas ;

the murder of Parmenion.

Parmenion stood for the old pan-Hellenic ideas.

328 Another Dionysiac revel at Maracanda. The murder of Cleitus.

Cleitus at the banquet protested against all the glory of the expedition being given to Alexander, instead of to the Macedonians.

The murder of Cleitus was justified for Alexander by the concept that the divine king can do no wrong.

The conspiracy of the pages.

The death of Callisthenes.

Callisthenes had protested against proskynesis and the orientalization of the monarchy.

Founding of Alexandreschata in the extreme north.

Plan to make an expedition to the far east to the Ganges and the Ocean.

Alexander turned from defeated ambition for being recognized as a god to world-domination.

326 The army rebelled at further advance.

Alexander yielded and set up an inscription : "Here Alexander stopped."

325 Three expeditions from the Indus to the land of Susa :
        of Craterus ;
        of Alexander ;
        of Nearchus.

Alexander devoted himself to exploration : military and naval achievements.

The expedition of Nearchus opened up an important economic route from the Indus to Susa.

Alexander had founded a maritime empire :
        including the valleys of the Nile, Tigris, Euphrates, Indus ;
        with Alexandria in Egypt the center of

commerce between East and West.

324 Grand nuptial fête at Susa.

Intermarriage between Greeks and Orientals was a step towards the foundation of an empire based on the brotherhood of man.

Creation of a division of indigenous cavalry.
Incorporation in the infantry of 30,000 native youths from all the provinces who had been taught Greek literature and military tactics.

Amalgamation of Greeks and barbarians.

324 Greek resentment at this caused the mutiny of Opis.
Death of Hephaestion.

324 Return to Babylon.
Sparta and Athens recognized Alexander as a god.

Alexander's divinity recognized by the Greeks.

323 Alexander died at Babylon.

His death ended his mystic dream of empire, established by force, then based on the ideas of the divine kingship, and the brotherhood of man.

APPENDIX II

In transcribing the Latin of the 1497 edition I have followed Oskar Hecker in *Boccaccio-Funde,* Brunswick, 1901, in making certain changes. I have modernized the punctuation, used a uniform system of capital letters (for example for proper names) and have expanded abbreviations. The quotations of poetry I have set off in lines for easier reading. In my translation, I have added in foot-notes references to quotations used by Boccaccio. I am indebted to Professor Cornelia C. Coulter for the original transcription of the passages from the *Genealogy.*

Boccaccio — De Genealogiis Deorum, *V.* 22 (*Venice,* 1497)
De Psyche. XV. Apollinis filia

Psyches ut dicit Martianus Capella in libro quem de nuptiis Mercurii et Philologiae scripsit filia fuit Apollinis et Endelichiae, ex qua Lucius Apuleus in libro Metamorphoseon, qui uulgariori uocabulo asinus aureus appellatur, longiusculam recitat fabulam talem. Regem scilicet fuisse et reginam, quibus tres fuere filiae, quorum duae maiores natu etsi forma spectabiles essent, iunior, cui Psyches nomen erat, in tantum pulchritudine caeteras excedebat mortales ut non solum admiratione teneret spectantes, sed infigeret animis ignaris rei miraculo credulitatem ut Venus esset, quae descendisset in terris ; et phama longe lateque vulgata invisae formositatis egit, ut non

solum cives sed exteri ad uisendam Venerem et sacris
honorandam accederent, templis uerae Veneris neglectis.
Quod aegre Venus ferens, in Psychen accensa, Cupidini
filio suo iussit ut eam amore ferventissimo hominis ex-
tremae sortis incenderet.   Interim pater de nuptiis Vir-
ginis Milesium Apollinem consuluit.   Qui respondit ut
illam in uertice montis deduceret, ibique diuina stirpe
creatum esto pessimum et uipereum nancisceretur uirgo
maritum.   Quo responso parentes affecti cum lachrymis
et maerore totius civitatis uirginem in praedestinatum
deduxere culmen, ibique solam liquere.   Quae etsi soli-
tudine et incerto timore futuri coniugis anxiaretur, non
tamen diu perstitit, et uenit Zephyrus mitis et suavi spiritu
eam assumens, in floridam detulit uallem, in qua cum
aliquali somno lenisset aerumnam, surgens uidit gratum
oculis nemus et argenteis undis manantem fontem, atque
palatium non solum regium, sed diuinum, miris ornatum
diuitiis.   Quod cum intrasset, et ingentes inuenisset the-
sauros absque custode, et miraretur plurimum obsequen-
tium uocibus absque corporibus auditis intravit lauacrum,
inuisis sibi assistentibus obsequiosis.   Inde coena divinis
conferta dapibus sumpta, cubiculum intrans, conscendit
genialem thorum et soporatae maritus affuit.   Qui cum
eam sibi fecisset coniugem, ueniente luce inuisus abiit, et
sic saepius magna Psychis consolatione continuans factum
est, ut sorores eiusdem audito Psychis infortunio e domi-
bus maritorum ad lugubres parentes accederent, et una
cum eis sororis infoelices nuptias deflerent.   At Cupido
praesentiens quid inuidia sororum pararetur Psychi, eam
praemonuit ut earum omnino flocci faceret lachrymas nec
in suam perniciem pia atque credula esset.   Quod cum
spopondisset Psyches, se coepit deplorare captivam et quod
sorores uidere et alloqui non posset, et uenientem atque
redarguentem Cupidinem praecibus in eam sententiam

traxit ut cum eis loqui posset Zephyroque iuberet ut eas
ad se leni deferret flatu. Qui cum fecisset concessit etiam
ut ex thesauris quos liberet asportare permitteret, sed
earum suasionibus nullo modo crederet nec suam uidere
formam alicuius consilio exoptaret. Tandem conplorata
domi Psyche a sororibus scopulum conscendere et ululatu
foemineo redintegrato a Psyche auditae sunt atque paucis
consolata verbis, et postremo illas Zephyrus Psychis im-
perio in uallem detulit amoenam. Ibi a Psyche festiua
congratulatione susceptae sunt eisque omnes ostensae
delitiae, ex quibus inuidae factae sorores ei totis suasere
nisibus ut uiri formam conaretur uidere. Quae credula
eis cum donis remissis novaculam parauit et lucernam
abscondit sub modio nocte sequenti uisura quisnam esset
is cuius uteretur concubitu, occisura eum si esset illi forma
uerbis sororum conformis. Intrat igitur more solito lec-
tum Cupido et in somnum soluitur. Psyches uero aperto
lumine uidit illum mira formositate conspicuum iuue-
nem, alis pernicibus insignitum, et ad eius pedes arcum et
pharetram sagittis confertam. Ex quibus cum unam
mirabunda eduxisset expertura aciem adeo digito impres-
sit suo ut aliqualis scaturiret e uulnere sanguis. Quo
facto miro dormientis adhuc amore flagrauit. Dumque
illum stupescens inspiceret, fauillula ex lucerna prosiluit
in dexterum dormientis humerum. Quam ob rem ex-
pergefactus Cupido repente fugam arripuit. Verum Psyches cum illum coepisset crure atque fortiter teneret,
tandiu ab eo per aerem delata est donec fessa eo dimisso
caderet. Cupido autem in uicinam cupressum euolans
longa querela eam redarguit se ipsum damnans quod a
matre missus, ut illam extremi hominis amore incenderet,
et ipse se ipsum ob eius pulchritudinem uulnerasset, et
inde euolauit. Psyches anxia perditi uiri mori uoluit.
Fraude tandem sorores ambas, quarum consiliis in ae-

rumnam uenerat, in praecipitium deduxit. Inde a Venere
obiurgata acriter et peditsequis eius lacessita uerberibus,
in labores mortali inexplicabiles iussu Veneris implicita,
opere uiri adiuta perfecit inuicta. Cuius postremo ad
Iouem precibus actum est ut in Veneris deueniret gratiam
et in caelis assumpta Cupidinis perpetuo frueretur coniugio. Cui peperit Voluptatem.

Serenissime rex si huius tam grandis fabulae ad unguem
sensum enucleare uoluerimus, in ingens profecto uolu-
men euaderet. Et ideo cur Apollinis et Endelichiae filia
dicatur Psyches, quae eius sorores, et cur Cupidinis dicatur
coniunx, cum paucis ex contingentibus dixisse satis sit.
Psyches ergo anima interpretatur. Hanc autem Apollinis, id est solis, filia dicitur, eius scilicet qui mundi uera
lux est deus, cum nullius alterius potentiae sit rationalem
creare animam nisi dei. Endelichia autem, ut dicit Calcidius super Thimeo Platonis, perfecta aetas interpraetatur.
Cuius omnino rationalis anima dicitur filia quia etsi in
utero matris illam a patre luminum suscipiamus. Non
tamen eius apparent opera nisi in aetate perfecta, cum
potius naturali quodam instinctu usque ad aetatem per-
fectam formamur quam iudicio rationis. Aetate vero
perfecta agere incipimus ratione. Ergo bene Apollinis
et Endelichiae filia dicitur. Sunt huic duae sorores,
maiores natu, non quia primo natae sint, sed quoniam
primo potentia utuntur sua. Quarum una uegetatiua
dicitur, altera uero sensitiua. Quae non animae sunt,
ut quidam uoluerunt, sed huius animae sunt potentiae.
Quarum ideo Psyches dicitur iunior quia longe ante eam
uegetatiua potentia conceditur foetui et inde tractu tem-
poris sensitiua. Postremo autem huic Psychi conceditur
ratio. Et quia primo in actu sunt immo primae dicun-
tur uinctae coniugio quod huic rationali diuinae stirpi
seruatur, id est amori honesto, seu ipsi deo. Cuius inter

delitias a Zephyro, id est a uitali spiritu, qui sanctus est
defertur et matrimonio iungitur. Hic coniugi prohibet
ne eum uidere cupiat ni perdere uelit, hoc est nolit de
aeternitate sua, de principiis rerum, de omnipotentia uidere per causas sibi quae soli notae sunt. Nam quotiens
talia mortales perquirimus, illum, immo nosmet ipsos
deuiando perdimus. Sorores autem nonnumquam ad
methas usque primas delitiarum Psychis deueniunt et ex
thesauris eius reportant in quantum penes rationem ui-
uentes. Melius opus suum uegetatio peragit. Et sensi-
tiuae uirtutes clariores sunt et longius perseuerant. Sane
inuident sorori, quod minime nouum est, sensualitatem
cum ratione discordem. Et dum illi blandis uerbis sua-
dere non possunt ut uirum uideat, id est uelit naturali ratione uidere quod amat, et non per fidem cognoscere, eam
terroribus conantur inducere, asserantes eum immanem
esse serpentem seque eam deuoraturum. Quod quidem
totiens sit quotiens sensualitas conatur rationem sopire et
ostendere animae contemplationem et cognitarum rerum
per causam, non solum delectationes sensitiuas auferre,
sed labores maximos, et angores minime opportunos in-
gerere, et nil demum placidae retributionis auferre. Anima autem dum minus prudens talibus demonstrationi-
bus fidem adhibet et quod negatur uidere desiderat occisura si uoto non correspondeat forma. Videt effigiem
uiri pulcherrimam, id est extrinseca dei opera. Formam,
id est diuinitatem, uidere non potest, quia deum nemo
uidit umquam. Et cum fauillula laedit et uulnerat, id
est superbo desiderio, per quod inobediens facta, et sen-
sualitati credula bonum contemplationis amittit, et sic a
diuino separatur coniugio. Tandem paenitens et amans
perniciem suorum curat astutia, easque adeo opprimit ut
aduersus rationem nullae sint illis uires et aerumnis et
miseriis purgata, praesumptuosa superbia atque inobe-

dientia, bonum divinae dilectionis atque contemplationis
iterum reassumit, eique se iniungit perpetuo, dum peri-
turis dimissis rebus in aeternam defertur gloriam. Et
ibi ex amore parturit uoluptatem, id est delectationem et
laeticiam sempiternam.

Boccaccio — De Genealogiis Deorum, *IX.* 4 (*Venice,*
1497)

De Cupidine primo Martis filio qui genuit Voluptatem
Cap. *IIII.*

Cupido, ut ait Tullius in libro de naturis deorum,
Martis et Veneris fuit filius, quem insipidi ueteres modern-
ique ingentis potentiae deum uolunt, quod satis patet
carmine Senecae tragedi, qui de (eo) in tragoedia Hyp-
politi :

Et iubet caelo superos relicto
Vultibus falsis habitare terras.
Thessali Phoebus pecoris magister
Egit armentum positoque plectro
Impari tauros calamo uocauit,
Induit formas quotiens minores.
Ipse qui celum nebulasque ducit,
Candidas ales modo mouit alas.

In quibus quam grandis sit potentia designatur.

Minus ostenditur in ea fabula quam de eo refert Ouid-
ius dum illum dicit ob Danis [1] pulchritudinem Apollinem Phitonis uictorem aurea uulnerasse sagitta et Da-
nem plumbea, ut amaret ille hanc, illa autem hunc haberet
odio.

Eius formam sic describit Seneca tragoedus in Octauia :

Volucrem esse amorem fingit inmitem deum
Mortalis error armat et telis manus

[1] for Daphnis.

Arcusque sacros [2] instruit seua face.
Genitumque credit credit Venere etc.

Seruius autem dicit eum aetate puerum, et Franciscus de Barbarino, non postponendus homo, in quibusdam suis pematibus vulgaribus huic oculos fascea uelat, et griphis pedes attribuit atque cingulo cordium pleno circundat.

Apuleius autem ubi de asino aureo eum describit formosissimum dormientem sic.   Cum uidelicet captis [3] aurei genialem caesariem, ambrosiam temulentiam, ceruices lacteas genasque purpureas perrantes [4] crinium globos decoriter impeditos, alios antependulos, alios retropendulos, quorum splendore nimio fulgurante, et ipsum lumen lucernae uacillabat ; per humeros uolatilis dei pennae roscide micanti flore candicant et quamuis aliis quiescentibus eximiae plumulae tenellae ac delicatae tremulae resultantes inquietae lasciuiunt.   Ceterum corpus glabellum atque luculentum et qualem peperisse Venerem non peniteret, etc.

Refert praeterea Ausonius ex hoc fabulam satis longo carmine scriptam quam pictam ait Treueris [5] in triclinio Zoili : Cupidinem scilicet inter mirteta herebi [6] casu euolasse, quem cum cognouissent heroides mulieres, eius ob causam dira suplicia et inhonesta desideria atque mortes passae, facto agmine, in eum confestim surrexere et frustra conantem exercere uires eum cepere, atque in excelsam ibidem mirtum cruci affixere suas inde pendenti ignominias iniicientes.   Quas inter dicit et aduenisse Venerem increpantem eum eique Vulcani cathenas inproperantem et supplicia seva minitantem.   Quibus commotis, aliis remissis suis iniuriis, a Venere ueniam illi impetrauere eumque sustulere de cruce et ipse euolavit ad superos.

---

[2] Read *Arcuque sacras,* as in the Loeb Text.
[3] capitis.
[4] perrantes.
[5] at Treves.
[6] Erebi.

Referuntur et insuper plura, quibus omissis dictorum perscrutandus est sensus.

Fuisse eum Cupidinem Martis et Veneris filium et insignem pulchritudine lasciuique moris satis possibile reor. Verum de hoc minime sensere fingentes et iccirco quis talis ex his oriri potuerit inter opiniones maiorum inuestigandum est. Est igitur hic, quem Cupidinem dicimus, mentis quaedam passio ab exterioribus illata et per sensus corporeos introducta et intrinsecarum uirtutum approbata praestantibus ad hoc supercaelestibus corporibus aptitudinem. Volunt namque astrologi, ut meus asserebat Venerabilis Andalo, quod quando contingat Martem in natiuitate alicuius in domo Veneris, in tauro scilicet vel in libra reperiri, et significatorem natiuitatis esse praetendere, hunc qui tunc nascitur futurum luxuriosum fornicatorem et uenerorum omnium abusurum et scaelestum circa talia hominem. Et ob id a philosopho quodam cui nomen fuit Ali in commento quadripartiti dictum est, quod quandocumque in natiuitate alicuius, Venus una cum Marte participat, habet nascenti concedere dispositionem philocationibus fornicationibus at luxuriis aptam. Quae quidem aptitudo agitur, ut quam cito talis uidet mulierem aliquam quae a sensibus exterioribus commendentur, confestim ad uirtutes sensitiuas interiores defertur quod placuit. Et id primo deuenit ad fantasiam, ab hac autem ad cogitationem transmittitur. Ab istis autem sensitiuis ad eam uirtutis speciem transportatur quae inter uirtutes apprehensiuas nobilior est, id est ad intellectum possibilem.

Hic autem receptaculum est specierum ut in libro de anima testatur Arist (oteles). Ibi autem cognita et intellecta si per uoluntatem patientis fit in qua libertas eiciendi et retinendi est ut tamquam approbata retineantur, tunc firmata memoria, haec rei approbate passio quae iam amor seu cupido dicitur, in appetitu sensitiuo ponit sedem. Et ibidem, uariis agentibus causis, aliquando adeo grandis et potens efficitur ut Iouem Olimpum linquere et tauri formam sumere cogat. Aliquando autem minus probata seu firmata labitur et annihilatur ira, et sic ex Marte et Venere non generatur passio sed, secundum quod supra dictum est, homines apti ad passionem suscipiendam secundum corpoream dispositionem producuntur, quibus non existentibus passio non generaretur. Sic large sumendo a Marte et Venere tamquam a remotiori paululum causa Cupido generatur.

Seneca autem tragoedus in Octauia ampliori paululum licentia, esto paucioribus uersibus, huius describit originem, dicens :

> Vis magna mentis, blandus atque animi calor,
> Amor et iuuenta gignitur luxu ocio nutritur,
> Inter laeta fortuna bona.

Sane in excusationem suae inbecilitatis hanc pestem mortales miseri pressi passione hac potentissimum finxere deum, quos in Hyppolito Seneca tragedus destatur dicens :

> Deum esse amorem turpi seruitio fauens
> Finxit libido, quoque liberior foret,
> Titulum furore numinis falsi addit, etc.

Sed iam eo ueniendum est ut, excussis fictionibus, quod sub eis sit absconditum uideamus. Hunc puerum fingunt ut aetatem suscipientium passionem hanc et mores designent. Iuuenes enim plurimum sunt, et more puerorum lasciuiunt, nec satis sui compotes, quo pasionis impellit impetu, potius quam quo ratio iusserit efferuntur. Alatus praeterea dicitur ut passio nati instabilitas demonstretur. Facile enim credentes cupientesque de passione

in passionem euolant. Arcum atque sagittas immo ferre
fingitur, ut insipientium reprentina captiuitas ostendatur,
nam in ictu fere oculi capiuntur. Has aureas esse dicunt
et plumbeas, ut per aureas dilectionem sumamus, quam
uti aurum lucidum atque preciosum est, sic et ipsa. Per
plumbeas autem odium uolunt, quod uti grave metallum
iners et uile fit, sic et maleuolentia reddit quos corripit.
Fax autem illi superaddita ostendit animorum incendia,
exustitione continua captiuos inconstantia. Oculos autem illi fascia tegunt, ut advertamus amantes ignorare
quo tendant, nulla eorum esse indicia, nullae rerum dis-
tinctiones, sed sola passione duci. Pedes autem gryphis
illi immo apponuntur, ut declaretur quam tenacissima
sit passio nec facile inerti impressa ocio soluitur. Eum
cruci affixum si sapimus documentum est, quod quidem
sequimur quotiens animo in uires reuocato laudabili
exercitio mollitiem superamus nostram et aptis oculis
perspectamus quoniam trahebamur ignauia.

De Voluptate filia Cupidinis. Cap. *V*.

Oluptas ut dicit Apuleius Cupidinis atque piscis [7] filia
fuit. Cuius generatoris fabula supra ubi de Psice latis-
sime dicta est. Cuius figmenti ratio aperietur facile.
Cum nam contingit nos aliquid optare ac optato potiri
procul dubio obtinuisse delectamur. Hanc delecta-
tioncm prisci Voluptatem uocauere.

[7] Psychis.

INDEX

A

Abdera, 14
Abradatas, 108
Abraham, 110
Achaia, 14, 89
Achilles, 14, 45, 46, 88, 105, 192
Achilles Romance, 46
Achilles Tatius, 58, 77, 91, 158
Acta, Christian, 90
Actaeon, 43
Acts of Andrew, 66
Acts of Paul, 66
Acts of Paul and Thecla, xi, 48-65, 76
Actus Petri Vercellenses, 66
Acts of Philip, 66
Acts of Thomas, 66
Acts of Xanthippe and Polyxena, xi, 48-80
Adlington, W., 120
Aegae, 86
Aeneid, 170, 171
Aeschines, 16, 41
Aeschylus, 173
Aesculapius, 86, 93
Aesop, 105
Aethiopica, of Heliodorus, 171
Africa, 11
Ajax, 14, 99
Alani, 3
Alcestis, 185
Alcibiades, 16
Alcmene, 43
Alexander, 4, 93, 106, 107, 191-95
Alexander the Great, The History of, xi, 1-47, 111
Alexander Romance, vii, xi, 46, 57
Alexander of Abonoteichus, 104
Alexander Severus, 84, 110
Alexander, the Syriarch, 53, 59, 64

Alexandreschata, 194
Alexandria, ix, 3, 11, 12, 30, 31, 33, 36, 39, 88, 192
Ali, 133, 203
Amazons, 26, 27, 32, 36, 41
Ammon, 5, 6, 8, 11, 23, 24, 29, 32, 33, 34, 36, 39, 93, 192
Amphion, 15, 43
Amphitryon, 43
Amyntas, 13
Amyot, J., 174
Anders, H. R. D., 172, 173, 174, 175, 182
Andrew, the apostle, 73, 74, 77, 79
Andromache, 105
Ante-Nicene Fathers, ix, 49, 50, 68
Anthia, 58, 82, 158, 159, 166
Antigone, 105
Antigonus, 24, 26, 29
Antioch, 11, 50, 52, 55, 56, 75, 84, 87, 144, 145, 156, 158
Antioch, Pisidian, 55, 56
Antioch, Syrian, 11, 55, 56, 87
Antiochus, King of Antioch, 144, 145, 146, 149, 156, 157, 158, 159, 160, 161, 180, 184, 185, 187
Antiope, 43
Antipater, 27, 35
Antonius Diogenes, 108
Aorne, 22
Aphrodite, 77, 106
Apocolocyntosis, 42
Apollo, 14, 16, 39, 57, 93, 125, 128, 131, 139, 148, 196, 199, 201
Apollo of Miletus, 126, 197
Apollonius of Tyana, vii, ix, xi, 81-112
Apollonius of Tyre, vii, xi, 142-71, 172, 175, 176, 178, 182
Apollonius of Tyre, vii, xi, 142-71, 184

207